"One of the most encouraging promises of the gospel of Jesus Christ is the promise of fresh starts and new beginnings. In this very helpful and practical book, Tim Lane not only helps you to understand that promise but shows you, step by step, how to experience that change in your own life and relationships. I can't imagine who wouldn't be helped by this book!"

Dr. Paul Tripp, Pastor; Author;
President, Paul Tripp Ministries

"We all at times find ourselves 'stuck' in familiar yet undesirable territory which we can't seem to change. As a coach, I [Clyde] appreciate how Tim has masterfully laid out nine steps to help us redirect our paths toward freedom and permanent heart change. *Unstuck* is an invaluable tool for all who long to break free from wrong and unwanted responses and, with the Spirit's help, see personal transformation toward living the full Christian life that God intended."

Clyde and Debbie Christensen,
Senior Offensive Assistant, Miami Dolphins

"Here's a wise, well-crafted, biblical plan for how we can pull up stubborn habits and sin patterns in our lives by the roots, and get rid of them once and for all."

Bob Lepine, Co-host, *FamilyLife Today*

"'Who we are comes before what we do.' This is good news for the person who desperately wants to change, and Tim's book is built on this solid foundation. *Unstuck* offers practical theology to the utmost—it's clever and compelling, and centers on Christ the whole way. I know I'll be returning to this book when I'm feeling stuck and want to see progress in specific areas of my heart and life."

Kristen Wetherell, Author, *Hope When It Hurts*

"All of us at some time (or many times) in our life have felt 'stuck.' We aren't growing; we seem to be repeating the same old behaviors and having the same old attitudes that harm our lives. Tim Lane insightfully and biblically helps us think through how we might get 'unstuck' and move forward in our lives and our relationship with Christ. *Unstuck* is full of wisdom and practical advice. I recommend it for all of us who find ourselves struggling to live in a way that moves us to a deeper relationship with God and others."

Tremper Longman III, Ph.D., Distinguished Scholar and
Professor Emeritus of Biblical Studies, Westmont College

"Just about every Christian gets stuck at some point in their Christian life. Here's a sound guide to getting out of the rut or the sludge, and finding the spiritual freedom needed to connect afresh with God and others. Christ-centered, biblically based, psychologically astute, and grace-oriented, this is a practical, but comprehensive help to live the life in Christ we were made for."

Eric L. Johnson, Ph.D., Senior Research Professor of Pastoral Care, Southern Baptist Theological Seminary

"*Unstuck* by Tim Lane has that rare, beautiful balance of a gospel-centered foundation and practical biblical principles for living out the gospel. *Unstuck* also combines relevant real-life illustrations, clear, creative content, and a workbook-like format that makes personal and ministry application doable."

Bob Kellemen, Ph.D., Author, *Anxiety: Anatomy and Cure*; V.P. and Academic Dean, Faith Bible Seminary

"Tim has done it again! He has written a readable, grace-filled, and 'practice-able' book that the reader will easily relate to. The clarity of the gospel is our guiding light as we consider a journey that begins with God's love and ends with us loving God and others. The message of *Unstuck* is both profound and simple... rich for the teenager and rejuvenating for the theologian."

Judy Dabler, MAC, MATS, Licensed Professional Counselor (Missouri); Certified Christian Conciliator; Founder, Creative Conciliation

"Tim has a wonderfully accessible and disarming way of inviting ordinary Christians who long to grow into significant spiritual reflection. His 9-step process is essentially a guide to experiential union with Christ, but it's not a quick-and-easy recipe—it's an invitation to take bold and courageous steps of self-awareness. This is a great gift to the church!"

Chuck Degroat, Ph.D., Professor of Pastoral Care and Christian Spirituality, Western Theological Seminary; Senior Fellow, Newbigin House of Studies; Licensed Professional Counselor, MI.

"This is a superb book for two primary reasons: 1) it accurately describes real-life situations which we Christians often face; and 2) it powerfully brings the word of God (both written and incarnate) to bear on those situations with practical, winsome, and effective grace. Thank you, Dr. Lane, for this book. I needed it!"

Dr. Samuel Logan, Associate International Director, The World Reformed Fellowship

"Although Scripture asserts that Christ has set us free, why do we have such trouble experiencing that freedom? Why do we worry and doubt? Why are we so easily consumed by anger and the urge to control things? Why are we unkind even toward the people we love most? Why do money and comfort drive us like they do? If you desire practical answers to these sorts of questions, if you feel tired of yourself and of your seeming inability to change, the book you hold in your hands is a potential lifeline. Both professionally and personally, Tim is a proven expert in gospel transformation. I can't recommend this book highly enough."

Scott Sauls, Pastor, Christ Presbyterian Church, Nashville, Tennessee; Author, *Jesus Outside the Lines* and *Irresistible Faith*

"*Unstuck* is a book I have been waiting for! Far too many Christians do not think deeply about their own continued growth. Tim Lane has given us a resource that is a clear, biblical, accessible, and comprehensive road map for personal change. It will help many be transformed into greater Christ-likeness."

Chap Bettis, Author, *The Disciple-Making Parent*; Executive Director, The Apollos Project

"What do you do when there is a particular sin you just can't seem to shake from your life? Tim Lane encourages us to work on ourselves, but always in the grounded assurance of God's character. In the gospel, we are united to the One who is loving enough to save us and powerful enough to transform us. Whether your problem is anger, lust, greed or gossip, *Unstuck* is the book to help you believe once more that change is possible."

Chris Cipollone, Founding Director, Biblical Counsellors Australia; Author, *Down, Not Out: Depression, Anxiety, and the Difference Jesus Makes*

"Tim Lane's *Unstuck* is an immensely practical and useful book for those struggling with life's challenges and those who counsel them. For those debating whether to see a counselor, it is an exceptional place to start, providing step-by-step guidance along a biblical path to growth. It is also a rich resource for Christian counselors to suggest to those who are 'stuck' in a tough place in life. Biblically rich and pastorally sensitive, *Unstuck* will be a gentle guide to many Christians."

Dr. Tim Sisemore, Licensed Psychologist; Author of 10 books including *Finding God While Facing Death*

TIM LANE
Unstuck
thegoodbook
COMPANY

For our parents
Clyde and JoAnn Lane
Bill and Sue Casey

Unstuck

Published by:
The Good Book Company

Email (US): info@thegoodbook.com
Email (UK): info@thegoodbook.co.uk

Websites:
North America: www.thegoodbook.com
UK: www.thegoodbook.co.uk
Australia: www.thegoodbook.com.au
New Zealand: www.thegoodbook.co.nz

thegoodbook COMPANY

ISBN: 9781784983680 | Printed in Denmark

Design by André Parker

CONTENTS

INTRODUCTION

Do you feel… *stuck*?

If you are reading this book, it is most likely because there is an area in your life that you want to change, but you don't know how to.

There's a behavior that you've tried to stop, but you just can't seem to do it.

There's a negative thought-pattern that you have attempted to move on from, but nothing you try ever works.

There's a relationship that you want to repair, but despite all your best intentions, nothing seems to make things better.

You want to change, but you feel… stuck. Maybe you can identify with one of the following people.

JONATHAN AND ANGER

Jonathan is a father of three. He used to be very easygoing, but lately he finds that the smallest thing can make him irritable and angry. Now he and his wife are struggling to get along. Every small decision becomes an argument, and they feel more and more distant from each other.

NANCY AND ANXIETY

Nancy struggles with anxiety. She, too, has made many attempts to change. She has applied helpful techniques she read online. She has raised the issue with her doctor and knows to seek medical advice when certain warning signs emerge. But the daily, low-level struggle continues. When Nancy reads the part of the Bible that says, "Do not worry," she feels hopeless. She can't imagine ever being free from her anxiety.

DAN AND ADDICTION

Dan has struggled with the same temptation for years. It started in his early teens. What seemed like fairly innocent viewing of a mildly suggestive website has become a lifestyle of addiction to pornography. He has tried countless times to change but to no avail. He doesn't even know where to begin. He is filled with guilt every time he fails, and his shame causes him to hide his struggle from others.

YOU?

Dan, Nancy, and Jonathan are normal people trying their best to navigate life and its challenges. They wake up every morning and face the same things you face: a difficult job, a challenging boss, financial pressures, physical ailments, past relational hurts, and a host of other things that are a part of life in a world that is both glorious and broken at the same time. Regardless, they get up every morning wondering if it could be better, and wishing that it could be.

Is it possible for them to respond to the challenges of life in ways that are hopeful and helpful?

Is it possible for them to break free from the habits and behaviors that don't seem to go away?

In other words, is it possible for them to get unstuck?

Yes, it is. And it's possible for you to get unstuck too.

DEEP AND PRACTICAL/OPTIMISTIC AND REALISTIC

This book will take you on a nine-step journey toward lasting change. I have spent many years counseling others through the change process (and decades seeking to grow as a Christian myself), and in that time I have found these nine steps to be essential to personal transformation. It's worth saying at the start that you will need all nine steps, not just a few—don't skip ahead or give up halfway through. In this book we'll seek to be both optimistic and realistic at the same time; we need to strike a balance between being optimistic about the hope for change and realistic about how hard and slow that change can often be.

These steps are much more than a simplistic technique: they are truths that are rooted in Scripture. Because of that, they are both deep and practical at the same time. Many books on change are truly deep. They plumb the depths of rich theology but remain detached from real life. They focus on right thinking. Other books get right to the issues and struggles that real people face. They are full of techniques and practical tips. They focus on right behavior, but often don't go deep enough for change to last .

This book will do both. We'll connect the rich truths of God's grace to the struggles of daily life that we all face. This is what is sometimes called "practical theology": theology that is practical and practice that is rooted in good theology.

As you journey through the various steps, you will notice that, at one level, they are not new. In fact, all theories and therapies are looking at the same key aspects of change. And there is a lot to learn from many current secular evidence-based therapies. But this book takes a distinctively Christian view of change. While there is much to learn from other theories, the Bible provides unique foundational truths that are essential to getting unstuck—that's why it will form the basis of every step on our journey.

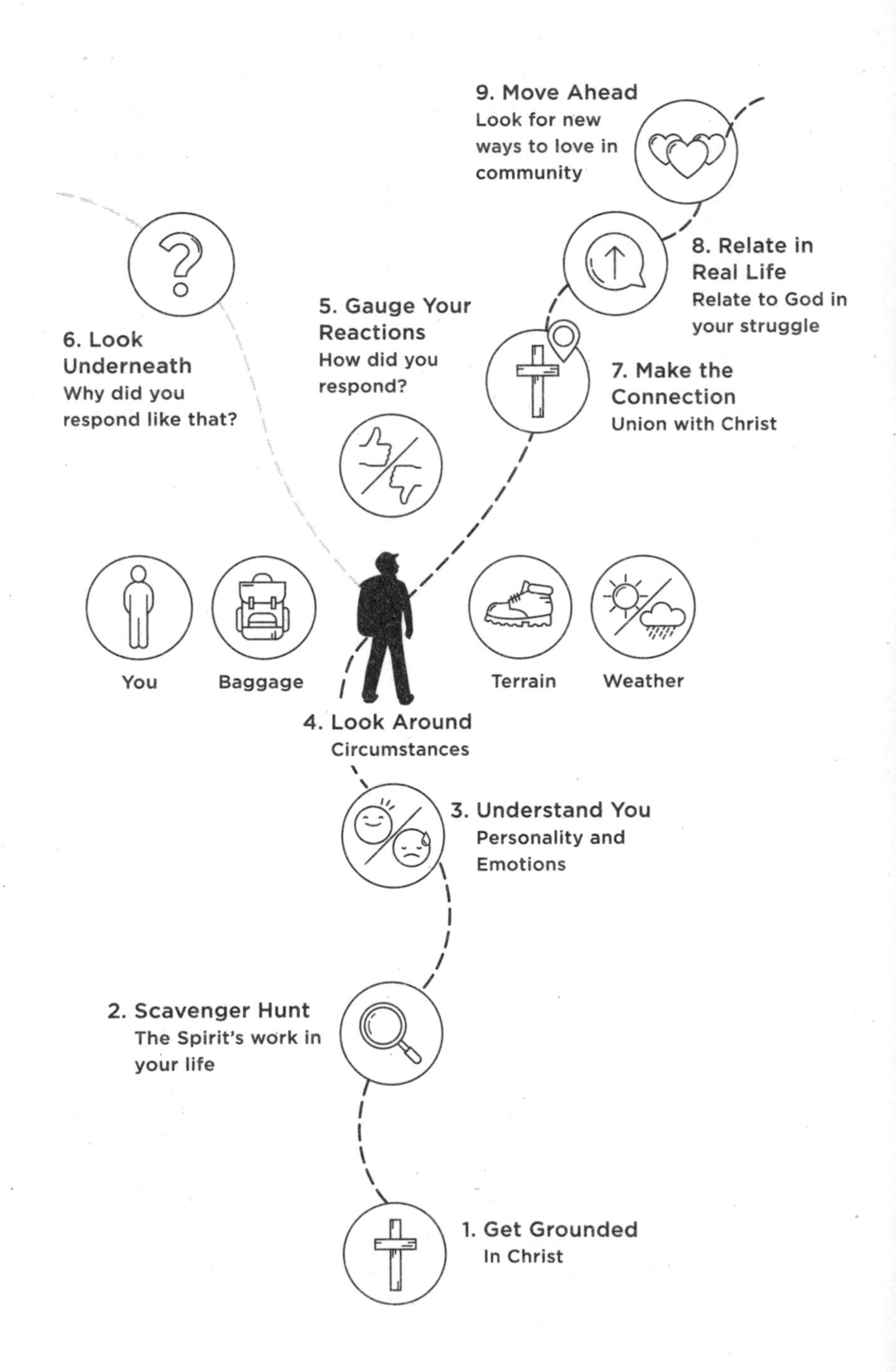
9. Move Ahead
Look for new ways to love in community
8. Relate in Real Life
Relate to God in your struggle
6. Look Underneath
Why did you respond like that?
5. Gauge Your Reactions
How did you respond?
7. Make the Connection
Union with Christ
You
Baggage
Terrain
Weather
4. Look Around
Circumstances
3. Understand You
Personality and Emotions
2. Scavenger Hunt
The Spirit's work in your life
1. Get Grounded
In Christ

WELCOME TO THE JOURNEY

Over the chapters that follow, we'll be imagining ourselves at a junction. The junction represents those pressure-point moments that we face every day. It could be anything: those moments when our kids are disrespecting us, or when our colleagues are disagreeing with us, or when temptation rears its ugly head. The question is: how do we respond?

If you're reading this book, it's probably because you feel stuck on the "left-hand track" of negative, unhelpful, and sinful attitudes and behavior. But in order to change your direction of travel—in order for you to choose the "right track" in the micro-moments—you need to see the junction as a whole. So the nine steps in this book will help you to look back along the road you've already traveled; consider why you so often take the left-hand fork; and, finally, show you how to increasingly do the right thing instead.

LET'S GET STARTED!

Before we begin with our first step, pick an area in your life where you would like to see change. Don't be discouraged. We all have areas of struggle. In fact, we all have more than one! But for the purposes of this journey, it helps to start by focusing on just one—the one that runs deepest or is having the biggest effect on your relationships. Write it in the space below:

AREA OF DESIRED CHANGE: ______________________________

If you can't think of anything, here are some suggestions:

- Is there something you tend to worry about? Finances, your job, a relationship?
- Is there something you tend to get angry about? Interruptions, other drivers, a certain type of person?

- Is there a typical way that you tend to escape when life gets hard? Watch TV, drink too much, eat for comfort?
- Do you tend to avoid conflict with others at all costs?
- Do you find yourself struggling with envy when you compare yourself to others? (Maybe with regards to appearance, material possessions, lifestyle?)
- Do you struggle with the "blues"? What do you get down about?
- Do you think a lot about material possessions and struggle to live within your means?
- Do you find yourself arguing with other people a lot?
- Is there a person or group of people that you have to have the approval of?
- Do you struggle with holding grudges and not being able to forgive someone?
- Do you struggle with fear? What is it that you fear? Rejection, getting a diagnosis from the doctor, losing your job?

If you have a hard time picking something, you could ask someone you trust to tell you where they think you need to grow. (But be careful who you choose!)

As we move along in our journey, you can keep coming back to this issue as a practical way to apply what you are learning in each chapter.

WHAT UNDERPINS THE POWER

Before we begin, there's one final thing to remember: all nine steps on this journey need to be underpinned by prayer. We cannot change ourselves; we need God to work in us by his Spirit. So start your journey of change by using this passage to pray and ask God for grace, encouragement, and strength to make progress.

I kneel before the Father, from whom every family in heaven and on earth derives its name. I pray that out of his glorious riches he may strengthen you with power through his Spirit in your inner being, so that Christ may dwell in your hearts through faith. And I pray that you, being rooted and established in love, may have power, together with all the Lord's holy people, to grasp how wide and long and high and deep is the love of Christ, and to know this love that surpasses knowledge—that you may be filled to the measure of all the fullness of God.

Now to him who is able to do immeasurably more than all we ask or imagine, according to his power that is at work within us, to him be glory in the church and in Christ Jesus throughout all generations, for ever and ever! Amen.
(Ephesians 3 v 14-21)

This short passage tells you so many wonderful things: you are loved by God, his power is at work in you, and he is with you and is able to help you as you seek to grow in grace.

Now, let's get started!

1. Get Grounded
In Christ

STEP 1
GET GROUNDED

Look back at what Christ has done for you.

Jim was a normal guy. He was married with children, had built his career, and was getting close to retirement. That was what I knew of him as we chatted one afternoon.

But I soon discovered that there was more going on under the surface. I had been doing some talks on anxiety, and as we talked, Jim revealed that worry had been his lifelong struggle. Later that week, he called and asked to start meeting with me one on one.

In our first two or three meetings together, I took my time to get to know him and his story. He had grown up as an only child with a verbally abusive father and a nurturing mother. He recounted years of teasing and bullying that he experienced throughout school and into college. This treatment had made him angry and pushed him in the direction of being a perfectionist. He made a vow that he would prove everyone wrong. He always made As on all of his exams. He was determined to show people that he was a successful person. And he was—four decades later, and Jim looked as if he had made it. Yet the treadmill had left him awash in a sea of depression and anxiety.

Jim was also a professing Christian. He was well thought of at church, had a firm grasp of theology, and understood the Bible better than most people. Yet what was most interesting about the way he told his story was that he rarely mentioned God. He made very few meaningful connections between his faith and his life. He didn't seem to see how Christ had given him the ability to maintain a good marriage and parent his children. He made no mention of God's grace, or Jesus' death and resurrection, or the work of the Holy Spirit as he recounted his life. In other words, Jim's story focused on one primary person: himself.

TIME TO TAKE STOCK OF THE PLAYERS

When you recount your history with all its challenges and triumphs, who are the most prominent players? From the way that you tell your story, would someone know that you have a vital dependence on Christ?

I have found in my own life and in the lives of those I counsel that this is the surest sign of whether someone is growing or stuck. When someone is growing, Christ is real. His presence and help are palpable. But when someone is stuck, the last person they talk about is Jesus. That is why this first step is so very important.

Before we can tell our story, and change our story, we need to take stock of who the players are. That's how it works in twelve-step recovery programs such as Alcoholics Anonymous. You probably know that the first thing someone in the program must do is admit that they have a problem: "My name is Tim and I am an alcoholic / compulsive gambler / sex addict." But it goes further than that—the participant must then acknowledge that they are powerless to overcome their problem and need a "higher power" to help them to change. This is no coincidence. Twelve-step programs owe this element to the early influence of the Christian faith. What has been proven through years of research is that people have a basic and utter need to start by looking away from themselves.

And so it is with you. When you stand at a junction and are faced with a moment of choice, the first thing you must do is to look back along the path. But unlike a twelve-step program, on this journey you don't look toward an impersonal force or a vague deity—you look to a person, and a day in history that has changed who you are forever. You look to Jesus.

GOODBYE TO GUILT

Here's why this step is so important. Whenever we start to see areas of struggle in our lives, it can immediately produce feelings of guilt and shame. Our gut instinct is to deny the problem and try to cover up the shame. We see this with Adam and Eve in the Garden of Eden. Upon their initial disobedience, they hid from God, covered themselves, and shifted the blame in an attempt to deal with their sense of guilt and shame before God.

Can you identify with this tendency? I can! When was the last time you failed at something or said something hurtful to someone? What did you immediately do? Pretend it wasn't that bad? Blame the other person? Just move on? The trouble is that none of these responses really deal with the situation or help us to change in the long term.

Over the course of this journey, you're going to be confronted with areas of sin and struggle in your own life. In order to resist the urge to hide, cover, and blame-shift in the face of your sin and suffering, it is so important to instead begin the change process in a place of confidence and safety.

You may be surprised to hear that this is actually what we find in the Bible. Whenever the biblical writers are addressing disobedience or calling believers to further obedience, they almost always start with emphasizing God's love and faithfulness to his people. For instance, consider how the Ten Commandments start. Before God gives the people of Israel his commands, he begins with these words in Exodus 20 v 2:

> *I am the LORD your God, who brought you out of Egypt, out of the land of slavery.*

That's amazing! God starts by reminding them of what he has already done for them. He had already saved them from slavery in Egypt, adopted them as his people, and promised to be with them every step of the way! It was only after this that he gave them the Ten Commandments. These commands were wise, good, and loving too. They weren't supposed to feel like a weighty burden but a natural way to express love and gratitude to God for his kindness. The Israelites didn't have to keep the Ten Commandments to earn their adoption and freedom; the rescue and adoption came first.

One of the most common errors in a Christian's life is forgetting this very important order: God's rescue leads to obedience. Obedience does not earn God's rescue. Who we are comes before what we do.

The apostle Paul follows a similar pattern in Philippians 2 v 1-4:

IDENTITY

> *If you have any encouragement from being united with Christ, if any comfort from his love, if any common sharing in the Spirit, if any tenderness and compassion...*

OBEDIENCE

> *... then make my joy complete by being like-minded, having the same love, being one in spirit and purpose. Do nothing out of selfish ambition or vain conceit. Rather, in humility value others above yourselves, not looking to your own interests but each of you to the interests of the others.*

Notice the pattern. Before Paul calls the Philippians to obedience in verse 2, he grounds them in their relationship with God in verse 1. It is only then that he says "then."

THIS IS WHO YOU REALLY ARE

The most profound resource that we have as Christians is a personal relationship with God where we enjoy his favor and love. Because of Jesus' life, death, and resurrection, we have a totally new identity and perspective.

Consider the following things that are true of you if you are a Christian. We will consider these truths in more depth later in the book, but it is worth noting them now. Paul says they are true of you because you are "in Christ."

- You are loved by God, and he chose to love you before you were even born (Ephesians 1 v 4-5).
- You are adopted as his child (v 5).
- You are freed from slavery to sin and your sins have been forgiven (v 7).
- You are in a lifelong relationship with God through Christ, and have been given the Holy Spirit, who is at work in you (v 13).
- You have a future hope of living in the very presence of God forever (v 14).

These are the blessings that Christ has secured for us through his life, death, and resurrection. It's what the Bible calls the gospel—the good news that people like you and me can be reconciled to God and have a new identity that is grounded in what Jesus has done for us.

Before we go any further, it's worth pausing to consider: is that what you believe? Where are you finding your identity? What are you relying on to make you right before God: your own efforts and good deeds, or what Jesus has done for you? That is a critical question to ask, because lasting change can only happen if you're "in Christ." If you aren't sure, speak to a Christian you trust and respect. And in the meantime, keep reading. I hope that as I describe the Christian vision of change, and what it means to be fully human, you will be compelled to genuinely put your trust and hope in the One who has made it possible through his life of perfect obedience, his death on the cross, and his resurrection from the dead—Jesus Christ.

JERRY AND SUSAN: THE GOSPEL IN REAL TIME

But how does this knowledge of who we are "in Christ" translate into our everyday life?

Jerry and Susan had been married for 20 years. They started struggling in their marriage about five years ago. A season of loss had opened doors for hurt and resentment to take over the tone of their marriage. They had been to several different counselors, and had been given various skills and techniques that did help their relationship. Yet there was always a challenge. What do you do when you are trying to love your spouse and they don't appreciate or notice? Unfortunately for Jerry and Susan, their attempts at change eventually led to greater hurt, frustration, and little hope that the marriage could be different.

As I began to work with them, I confirmed that many of the skills they had been given were indeed very helpful. In fact, they had probably helped them stay married for this long. But we needed to go deeper. After getting to know them better, I began to help them make connections with who they were in Christ.

Over several months we discussed Philippians 2 v 1-4 during our meetings. I gently guided them to ponder this passage. Here is what the conversation sounded like:

- "Jerry and Susan, tell me where you have experienced 'any encouragement from being united with Christ' this past week. Have you found encouragement in the fact that your sins have been forgiven and that God completely accepts you? From the truth that he doesn't just tolerate you but really loves you deeply?"
- "Jerry and Susan, talk to me about how you have experienced 'any comfort from his love' this week. Life is hard and relationships are challenging, but God desires to comfort you in the midst of your struggles—even struggles in your marriage."
- "Jerry and Susan, paint a picture for me of a time this week when you have experienced 'any common sharing in the Spirit.' When did you not do what seemed natural, but instead found new power to react to life differently? Did that happen between the two of you?"
- "Jerry and Susan, how have you experienced God's 'tenderness and compassion'? What was that like? How did you feel?"

After several weeks of talking about these things, Jerry and Susan began to think about it more carefully throughout the week. Some weeks they would come in with rich and vivid memories of being on the receiving end of God's grace and kindness. Some weeks they wouldn't have much to say. But what became clear was that in the weeks when they did see how they had experienced God's compassion, kindness, forgiveness, and grace, they would report that their relationship seemed better. Granted, it wasn't perfect.

But they were beginning to look up, and that was changing them and their marriage. You could call this "Christian mindfulness"—Jerry and Susan were becoming more mindful of their relationship with Jesus in the moment, not just when they were at a worship service in a church.

When Jerry and Susan were growing more deeply in their identity as adopted children of the Father, they discovered a new desire and ability to be humble—recognizing their own failings and not just pointing a finger at each other. They started to think less of what they needed and more of what the other one needed. And when they did have a need, they were learning how to express that to one another graciously instead of making demands.

The same effect can be seen in any personal struggle. Whether your struggle is with worry, addiction, discouragement, anger, fear, or anything else, starting with who you are in Christ is foundational—because God's compassion and grace toward us always comes before his wise and loving commands. This is one of the unique aspects of the Christian faith.

God's love for us is always first. His wise and loving commands are second. We are loved in Christ so that we might obey him. We don't obey him so that we might win his love.

WORK IT THROUGH

With this biblical backdrop in mind, let's start to get very practical. Locate a few passages which remind you that you belong to God and that you are secure in his gracious and loving embrace. Take a moment to find a few passages that are particularly relevant for the area of struggle you chose at the beginning of your journey. If you're not sure where to start, ask someone you trust to help you find some passages together.

PASSAGE 1: ______________________________

PASSAGE 2: ______________________________

PASSAGE 3: ______________________________

Don't stop there. Select the most helpful passage and put it in a place where you can easily access it: on your phone, in a notebook, on your refrigerator. Whenever you see those verses, talk to God and thank him for how he has loved you.

Are there other ways to meditate on God's love for you? Is there a favorite song or hymn that reminds you of his grace? A poem? A phrase? A work of art? A friend who tells you the Great News whenever you see them? Take a moment and write that down.

HYMN OR SONG: ______________________________

POEM, PHRASE, OR WORK OF ART: ________________

A FRIEND: ______________________________

WHAT IS HAPPENING?

As you think about the struggle that you chose at the beginning of this book, what was your experience when you first wrote it down? Guilt? Embarrassment? Despair? Now that you have turned your gaze to Jesus, how do you feel? Can you see why this first step is so vital to getting unstuck from your struggle and moving forward?

So often we listen to the voice of our conscience, which whispers words of guilt, shame, and condemnation. These thoughts hum in the background of our minds like white noise and prevent us from hearing the clear sound of God's voice. You must fight to replace the voice of this false narrator with that of the true Narrator, who speaks the truth about who you are and to whom you belong. He says this about you in Romans 8 v 1: "Therefore, there is now no condemnation for those who are in Christ Jesus."

Take a moment and sing the song or read the passage out loud. You have taken the first and most vital step on the journey to lasting change! This first step is one that you must keep coming back to every day, and in every moment of every day. Don't let it fade into the background.

KEEP RUNNING

As we begin the process of self-examination in this book, it must begin by looking outward—at Jesus. Our instinct is to begin by looking at ourselves. But the Bible tells us that change begins as we gaze outward and away from ourselves:

> *Let us throw off everything that hinders and the sin that so easily entangles. And let us run with perseverance the race marked out for us, fixing our eyes on Jesus, the pioneer and perfecter of faith. For the joy set before him he endured the cross, scorning its shame, and sat down at the right hand of the throne of God. Consider him who endured such opposition from sinners, so that you will not grow weary and lose heart.* (Hebrews 12 v 1-3)

As you continue on this journey, you'll soon discover that change is like a marathon. It's hard work. There's a lot of sweat. It's exhausting. Sooner or later you'll feel that you've hit "the wall." But Jesus has blazed a trail before you. He endured the cross in order to guarantee that you'll reach the finish line. So fix your eyes on him and on what he has done for you—not just today but every day. It's by looking to him that you'll find the strength to keep on running.

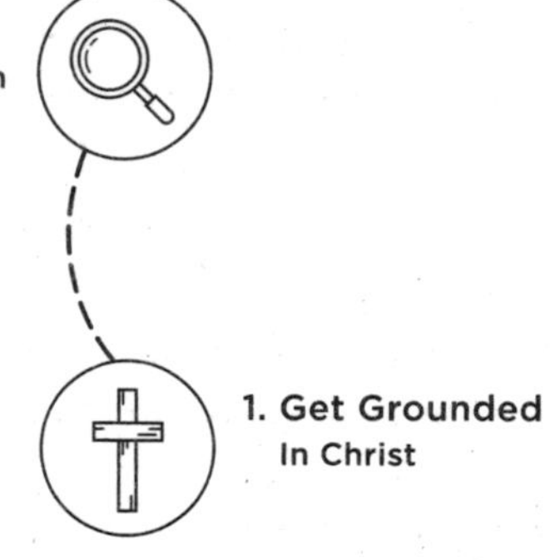
2. Scavenger Hunt
The Spirit's work in
your life
1. Get Grounded
In Christ

STEP 2
SCAVENGER HUNT

Look for evidence of the Spirit's work in you.

Have you ever been on a scavenger hunt with kids in the outdoors? Suddenly you start taking notice of all the things that passed you by before—every leaf or weed or insect takes on a new significance! Why? Because you're looking for them.

Our next step involves doing something similar—we're going on a spiritual scavenger hunt.

A TYPICAL MARRIAGE?

Rob and Erin came to me for marriage counseling. They seemed like your average Christian couple, but as I began to get to know them, I discovered that their background was a little more complicated. Both had come from severely broken homes and had lived lives of confusion and self-destruction before they eventually became Christians, met one another, and got married.

Now they were telling me how hard it was for them to get along. They had several small children, were starting a business together, and were trying to navigate ongoing extended-family fallout over a host of issues.

I asked them to tell me about their marriage. Here is what they described:

- We are not communicating and getting along.
- We are constantly fighting with one another.
- We are not working as a team.
- We are such a poor example of a Christian marriage.
- We are doing the same things to our kids that were done to us.
- Are we heading for a divorce just like our parents?
- Does God really love us in light of the way we are responding to one another?

As I got to know them over several months, I did see some of the things they saw, but I also saw something very different:

- A married couple made up of two sincere Christians.
- A couple who wanted their marriage to last.
- A couple who were seeking outside help, again.
- Rob really cared for Erin and wanted to encourage her.
- Erin really cared for Rob and wanted to encourage him.
- They were involved in a small group with other couples.
- They were avid readers of books and listeners of podcasts that pointed them to Christ.
- They had been married for eight years.
- They loved their children and pointed them to Christ.
- They served others within the context of their church.
- They longed to love their extended family well.

Do you see how starkly different those two lists are? The contrast couldn't be greater!

John and Erin did not see what I saw. Yet the very fact that they were seeking help was a mark of the Spirit ablaze in their lives!

WHY YOUR GLASS IS HALF FULL

This is very typical for people who are going through a difficult season. There are two kinds of blind spots. One is to be blind to our sin. Another is to be blind to the Spirit at work in our lives. You might compare it to being either a glass-half-full or glass-half-empty kind of person.

While some people are oblivious to their weaknesses, my experience is that *most* people who come to me for counseling tend to see the "glass" half empty. They start with the negative. Here is the self-talk that is often going on in their own minds: "What is wrong with me? Why do I continue to do things that I should not do, and why don't I do the things I should? I'll never be able to change. I bet no one else on the planet struggles with this." That negative voice or inner critic is usually the voice of guilt and shame, not the Spirit.

How about you? When you take a good look at your life, what is your tendency? Is it to gloss over your weaknesses or to beat yourself up over them (or do both, depending on the situation)? Do you struggle to see where you are going wrong? Or are you so preoccupied with your failures that you can't see how God is already changing you for the better?

When the former is happening, that is the slippery voice of self-delusion—we'll address that particular blind spot with Steps 5 and 6. But when the latter is happening, that is the destructive voice of guilt and shame. It must be confronted with the convincing and encouraging voice of the Spirit. That's what this chapter will help you with.

A FIGHTING CHANCE

Step 1 on our journey to change was to look back along the path to Christ: at what he has done, and who he has made you to be "in him" when you became a Christian. These are spiritual realities that Scripture assures us are true.

The next step is to look back at all the ways the Spirit has changed you since then, and how he is continuing to work in you today. This is an important step because many of us are prone to focus on our faults and failures, not on Spirit-wrought perseverance and good fruit. Then we'll become discouraged. Or on the other hand, if we focus on our own moral victories or triumphs of will-power, we'll become proud if we do not recognize that all the good we do comes from the Spirit.

Once again, Scripture changes our gaze. The apostle Paul was not in denial about the reality of sin. Yet his New Testament letters to Christians are always powerfully optimistic about the way that the Spirit is on the move in the lives of those who belong to Christ. Here's how he addresses the church in Philippi:

> *I thank my God every time I remember you. In all my prayers for all of you, I always pray with joy because of your partnership in the gospel from the first day until now,* ***being confident of this, that he who began a good work in you will carry it on to completion until the day of Christ Jesus.*** *(Philippians 1 v 3-6)*

If you have heard and believed the gospel, then God has begun a good work in you by his Spirit. From this passage, and the New Testament as a whole, we can conclude three amazing things about the work of the Holy Spirit in us:

First, the Holy Spirit is God. He's not some kind of force or a fairy godmother. He is the third Person of the Trinity, equal to the Father and the Son. That makes his presence within us both extraordinarily powerful and deeply personal. That is what Paul means when he says that God himself has begun a good work in the Philippians. Today, as you read this, you have the triune Lord of the universe living and working in you through the person of the Holy Spirit. It's impossible to overstate what an astonishing truth this is!

Second, the Holy Spirit shows that you belong to God. The Holy Spirit dwells in every believer, and so his work in your life is evidence that you belong to God (Ephesians 1 v 13). Even when you mess up badly, or are agonized by temptation, the very fact that you call out to God as your Father is a work of the Spirit—it shows that he is still working in you and that you belong to God.

Third, the Holy Spirit will not give up. The Holy Spirit is at work in you, changing you, and will not stop until you reach the finish line: heaven. God will carry this work "on to completion" (Philippians 1 v 6). You have what you need to change—and the evidence of that is what he's already doing. God has not, and will not, give up on you. His goal is to conform you into the very likeness of Jesus so that you display his perfect character more and more.

There is a place for addressing the ongoing battle with our failures, weaknesses, and remaining sin—but for now, rejoice in the fact that you are in the fight! While it may not be easy, the fact that you are battling sin is evidence that you are spiritually alive.

HOPE FOR HOPELESS CASES

This is true even in the most hopeless cases. The church in first-century Corinth certainly looked like one of those. It was full of problems—and not little ones, either. We're talking about incestuous relationships, dirty church politics which led to intense rivalries, Christians suing one another, and deep divisions along economic lines. In view of all that, Paul begins his letter to them in this way:

> *To the church of God in Corinth, to those sanctified in Christ Jesus and called to be his holy people, together with all those everywhere who call on the name of our Lord Jesus Christ—their Lord and ours: Grace and peace to you*

> *from God our Father and the Lord Jesus Christ.* ***I always thank my God for you because of his grace given you in Christ Jesus. For in him you have been enriched in every way—with all kinds of speech and with all knowledge—God thus confirming our testimony about Christ among you.*** *Therefore you do not lack any spiritual gift as you eagerly wait for our Lord Jesus Christ to be revealed. He will also keep you firm to the end, so that you will be blameless on the day of our Lord Jesus Christ. God is faithful, who has called you into fellowship with his Son, Jesus Christ our Lord.* *(1 Corinthians 1 v 2-9)*

Astonishing! That is not the way I would begin a letter to a church like this. But if my eyes were searching for signs of the Spirit's work, I might. Paul does go on to address the deep problems in the church, but notice where he begins. This is a typical pattern in almost all of Paul's letters to the churches. Even where he has deep concerns, he still sees and acknowledges the work of the Spirit in them. And if that was true for a church like Corinth, that can be true for a Christian like you.

HOW DO YOU SEE CINDY?

Now let's consider how this should change the way we view other believers, including ourselves. Cindy is a friend of mine. I have known her for over a decade. We go to church together. She has battled depression for her entire adult life. Most Sundays, I see her in the worship service. Sometimes I can see that she is singing with a degree of joy; other Sundays she just sits in her seat as others around her stand and sing.

At first glance, you might be tempted to be judgmental and conclude that Cindy lacks faith. But recalibrate your perspective of Cindy by following Paul's example.

When we do that, we can see that there are obvious signs of the Spirit at work in her life. She continues to stay connected to her church. She continues to acknowledge her dependence upon Christ. She desires for her neighbors to know Jesus. She shares her faith with others in her family. She seeks helpful counsel from friends. She sees a counselor on a regular basis. When we begin to acknowledge these things, we start to see Cindy in a very different light. These are remarkable marks of the Spirit on the move in her life!

More than likely, Cindy will be the last to see these things. And you will too if you look only at her faults and failures. The same is true when we look at ourselves. Change is fueled by hope, and hope emerges when you can see that God is actively at work in you and that he has not abandoned you!

WORK IT THROUGH

Do you see how very important it is to begin with a vision of God's presence and work in your life? Without this truth and perspective, you will tend to only see what is wrong in your life and not the good things that God is doing through the Spirit. Let's take this perspective and get very practical.

Go on a scavenger hunt for evidence of the Spirit's work in your life. Be as meticulous as a good detective. As you consider various areas of your life, look for any and every evidence of the Spirit's work, no matter how small. Let this move you in the direction of gratitude. *Be utterly thorough about this.* Let me prime the pump to help you get started.

- If you have struggled with the same old temptation and are still in the fight, that is a mark of the Spirit.
- If you have been fighting an addiction, and you have invited another person to hold you accountable, that is a mark of the Spirit.

- If you have said or done something to hurt another person, and you desire to confess your offense and ask for forgiveness, that is a mark of the Spirit.
- If you have been struggling with depression for years, but you stay connected to the body of Christ and you occasionally think about reading your Bible or praying, that is a mark of the Spirit.
- If you are married, and you are still desiring a good marriage and seeking good counsel, that is a mark of the Spirit.
- If you have given of your time and other resources and didn't expect to be acknowledged or repaid, that is a mark of the Spirit.

These are confirmations that you belong to God and that his Spirit is working in you. Never despise the simple signs of his presence in your life. I use the word "never" not to shame you but to encourage you!

Be practical. Get out a piece of paper and start pondering every evidence of God's work in your life. Don't stop until you can list 25 things.

If you are having trouble, ask a trusted friend to help you. Sometimes other gracious people can see evidence of God's work in you better than you can. Maybe you can do the same for them. Make it an occasion to encourage one another.

ONE MORE PIECE OF EVIDENCE

Why are these first two steps so important? Because they get you looking in a better direction. It is easy to let your circumstances and your failures weigh you down, turn you inward, and make you feel stuck. These first two steps move in a very different direction and provide a solid foundation for you to take the next steps that will follow.

But don't miss what you have already done. In fact, here's one final evidence of the Spirit's work to add to your list, if you haven't got it already: you are reading this book! And you've already made it to the end of chapter two. More importantly, you have started to change your perspective by looking outward to see Jesus and his work in your life.

That is revolutionary. It is miraculous. It is evidence that you are growing. Be encouraged!

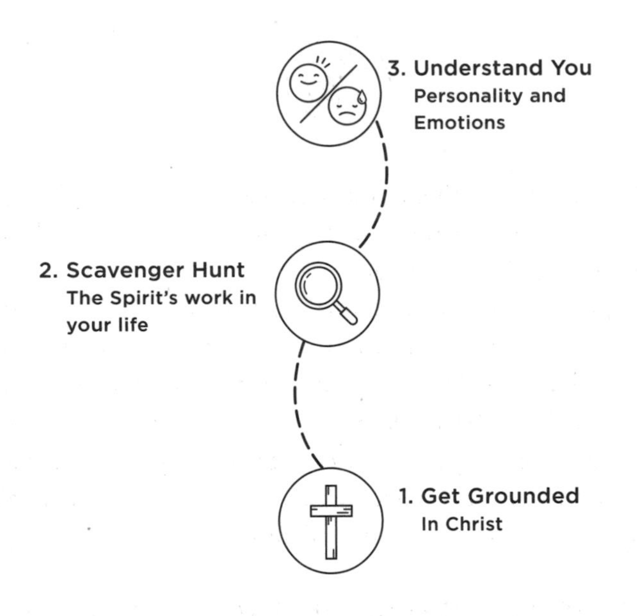
3. Understand You
Personality and
Emotions
2. Scavenger Hunt
The Spirit's work in
your life
1. Get Grounded
In Christ

STEP 3
UNDERSTAND YOU

Rightly understand your personality and emotions, and how this relates to change.

You're reading this book because you want to change. But in this chapter we'll consider: What is it about you that actually *can* change?

Our personality and emotional makeup are two important aspects of who we are. Each of us is uniquely different, and most of these differences are hard-wired into us due to our DNA, which has been passed on to us by our parents. That means that these aspects *don't* change; and, as we'll see, they don't *need* to change. They do need to be managed wisely though; that's what this step is all about.

BUSINESS PARTNERS/DIFFERENT PERSONALITIES

Joseph and Stuart were business partners. Stuart was great at sales and Joseph handled all the systems to keep up with the data: the clients, income, expenses, and profit. The two of them worked well together for the first five years and the business was booming. But something started to change. Whereas they used to always have each other's back, soon the relationship began to crumble. There were little resentments and frustrations that became more pronounced. Joseph would get frustrated with Stuart because he didn't appreciate all the hard work Joseph was doing in the office. Stuart began to get frustrated with Joseph because he never seemed very excited when Stuart landed a new client. Stuart was loud and funny, and the life of the party, while Joseph was more reserved and would often go unnoticed. Resentment grew. Several years later, Joseph tried to push Stuart out of the business and they eventually wound up in a lawsuit.

MARRIED COUPLE/DIFFERENT EMOTIONS

Mike and Sena have been married for ten years. Mike grew up in a home where he never saw any conflict between his parents. They were always very rational when they had a disagreement. Mike believes that emotions get in the way of good relationships and that they should be expressed very carefully. Sena, on the other hand, grew up in a family where she was encouraged to embrace and express her emotions in appropriate ways. It was safe to be sad, happy, angry, or excited.

When Mike and Sena were dating, they were naturally drawn to one another. Mike loved how Sena was so vivacious and outgoing. Sena loved how Mike was always calm and clear-headed.

But after a decade of marriage, the very thing that had drawn them together was now tearing them apart. Whenever Mike and Sena got into an argument, Mike would tell Sena to calm down and put a lid on her emotions. This would make Sena very angry and upset. Whenever Sena was angry, Mike would shut down and just walk away. Sena would say, "I hate it when you walk away. It feels like you are cutting me out of your life." Mike would reply, "Well, if you would get a handle on your emotions, maybe I wouldn't walk away!"

PERSONALITY ON THE PAGE

Your personality and emotional makeup are part of the unique and wonderful way that you have been created by God. As such, much of our personality and emotional makeup is present from birth, but they can also be shaped as we grow up. Most parents will attest to that.

While the Bible does not speak in terms of personality per se, it does paint pictures of very unique individuals. Some personalities bleed through the pages of Scripture more than others.

Consider the apostle Peter. Whenever Jesus asks a question, Peter is often the one who speaks up. He's the first disciple to blurt out that Jesus is the Christ (Matthew 16 v 13-20). He's the only disciple who initially refuses to let Jesus wash his feet (John 13 v 6-9). In the Garden of Gethsemane, he's adamant that he will lay down his life for Jesus—but it turns out he's all talk (v 31-38). Through all his faults and failings, we get the distinct impression from the Gospel accounts that Peter is an expressive, outgoing guy!

Likewise, in Scripture we find dialogue and poetry that are rich in emotions. Just consider the Psalms. In many places you see joy, gladness, happiness, and other positive emotions. Other psalms are filled with negative emotions like fear, sadness, anger, and lament. Psalm 88 ends on a dark note:

> *You have taken from me friend and neighbor—darkness is my closest friend.* (v 18)

This is followed by Psalm 89 which begins this way;

> *I will sing of the LORD's great love forever; with my mouth I will make your faithfulness known through all generations.* (v 1)

From the end of one psalm to the beginning of another we move from deep despair and loneliness to great joy, thanksgiving, and praise. The Psalms, and many other parts of the Bible, remind us that emotions are a central part of life. It is a fundamental part of being human!

All this is very consistent with the teaching of Psalm 139:

> *For you created my inmost being; you knit me together in my mother's womb. I praise you because I am fearfully and wonderfully made; your works are wonderful, I know that full well. My frame was not hidden from you when I was made in the secret place, when I was woven together in the depths of the earth. Your eyes saw my unformed body; all the days ordained for me were written in your book before one of them came to be.* (v 13-16)

One writer says this about these verses:

> *The words "knit together" and "woven together" are terms that refer to the complex patterns and colors of a weaver or embroiderer ... You ... were created in infinite wisdom and love, and you reflect [God's] image ... Your design was set and your days were determined by the hand of God, the Master Weaver.*
>
> *But there's more here. The psalmist also talks about his "frame" or "bones." One highly respected commentator asserted that the word means "strengths." This author translated the word to mean "potentialities" or "capabilities." Think about that. When God made you, he placed within you natural strengths and abilities. He wove those into the fabric of your inner being. And those capabilities and potentialities are part of your unique design. They were given to you to be used to accomplish things for him.*
>
> (Dr. Charles F. Boyd, *Different Children, Different Needs*, p 26-27)

If our personality and emotional makeup are woven into us by God, it means that these patterns are inherently good. Our differences in this area are to be celebrated.

So does this excuse the sinful ways in which we treat others? Should we just accept that an "angry person" will always get angry, or that a "controlling person" will always manipulate others?

No. It's crucial to understand that there is a difference between your personality and your character. Your *character* changes through the ongoing process of sanctification. Your personality is the lens through which your character is expressed—so the aim is to use your personality to increasingly express and reflect Christ-like character. Exactly how this looks will vary from person to person depending on their personality; but this is something we do need to think wisely about. As you seek to grow in character, it helps to first understand your personality.

UNDERSTANDING YOUR PERSONALITY

So how can we begin to understand our own personality better? There are many personality assessments, but one that I have found to be most helpful is the Birkman Method, developed in the 1940s by Roger Birkman and now used internationally. Since it is much more nuanced and complex than I will explain here, you can find out more online (www.birkman.com or www.timlane.org/the-birkman-method). In this chapter we'll focus on two aspects: the Birkman Map and the Birkman Components.

First, the Birkman Map shows four basic personality types (look it up online to see it in color!):

- *Extroversion:* someone who is more expressive verbally, emotionally and behaviorally.
- *Introversion:* a person who is less expressive verbally, emotionally and behaviorally.

- *Task Orientation:* a person who tends to be more focused on finishing tasks and projects.
- *People Orientation:* a person who tends to be more focused on working with others and forming connections.

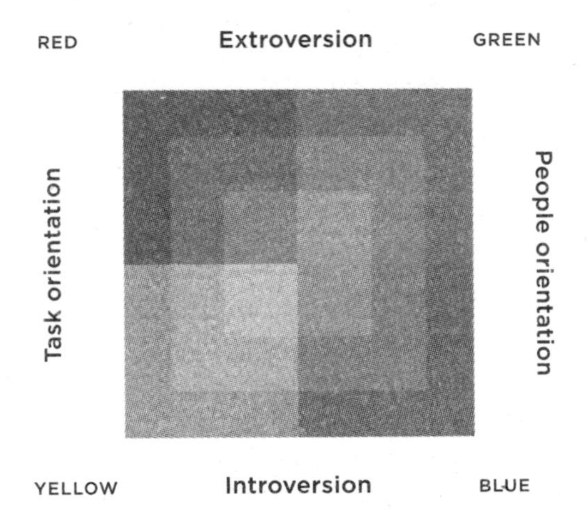

Second, there are nine Birkman Components that measure personal and interpersonal behavior. Each component has a score range from 1-99. No score is good or bad—it just is. The higher or lower the score, the more predictable one's behavior will be. When the score is in the middle (40-60), a person may respond either way depending on the situation. Understanding these is critical to understanding your own and other people's personalities.

- *Social energy:* your sociability, approachability, and preference for group and team participation.
  Low scores: more independent.
  High scores: more sociable.
- *Physical energy:* your preferred pace for action and physical expression of energy.
  Low scores: more efficient.
  High scores: more active.

- *Emotional energy:* your openness and comfort with expressing emotions.
  Low scores: more practical.
  High scores: more expressive.
- *Self-consciousness:* your use of sensitivity when communicating with others.
  Low scores: more candid.
  High scores: more tactful.
- *Assertiveness:* your tendency to speak up and express opinions openly and forcefully.
  Low scores: more suggesting.
  High scores: more directing.
- *Insistence:* your approach to detail, structure, follow-through, and routine.
  Low scores: more flexible.
  High scores: more consistent.
- *Incentives:* your drive for personal reward or preference to share in group reward.
  Low scores: more collaborative.
  High scores: more competitive.
- *Restlessness:* your preference for focused attention or varied activities.
  Low scores: more focused.
  High scores: more responsive.
- *Thought:* your decision-making process and concern for consequences in making the right decisions.
  Low scores: more decisive.
  High scores: more reflective.

You are a unique combination of all nine components. There is no right or wrong; moral or immoral; good or bad. It is just who you are. The goal of the Birkman Assessment is to help people understand and embrace differences before they lead to unhelpful conflict. It also helps you see that your normal way of doing things may not always be the best way in every situation.

BACK TO JOSEPH AND STUART

Joseph and Stuart are very different. Joseph is an introvert and needs time to focus so that he can get his work done. He is a natural at details, systems, and keeping up with data. A large part of who Joseph is is represented in the bottom left (yellow) section of the Birkman Map. (In terms of the Birkman Components, he is probably a combination of lower social energy, lower physical energy, higher insistence, lower restlessness, and higher thought.)

Stuart, on the other hand, is an extrovert and is drawn to people. He loves selling things and convincing people that they need the product that he is representing. Stuart's personality would show up in the top right (green) section of the Birkman Map (possibly a combination of higher social energy, higher physical energy, lower self-consciousness, lower insistence, higher incentives, higher restlessness, and lower thought).

It was these differences that made their business successful. Stuart left the office and spent time with people selling the product, while Joseph stayed in the office and kept up with the details. These personality types are good. Joseph and Stuart are stronger and weaker at different things, but there is nothing inherently sinful in the way that they get things done.

However, at some point Joseph and Stuart started being critical of each other's weaknesses, and feeling that their strengths weren't being appreciated by the other. Their differences led to misunderstanding, which led to uncharitable perceptions and attitudes. This uncharitable perception led to sinful pride, criticism, and defensiveness. Had they known how their differences were a good thing, they could have avoided the conflict. Now, if Joseph and Stuart were going to continue to work together, they would need to admit and confess their sinful attitudes and actions toward each other, and forgive one another. But they would also need to understand their different personalities, strengths, and ways of getting things done, in order to move forward.

Something similar can happen in all of our relationships. Because of sin, we can become proud and elevate our personality over others. This leads to personality bias, misunderstanding, and conflict. Here is what it sounds like:

- My way is the only way to get things done.
- My way is the only way to feel about something or someone.
- I am normal and others are abnormal.
- My personality is the ideal personality.
- Things would go better if others conformed to my way.

God's grace, though, can keep us humble so that we remain charitable. Here is what that might sound like:

- My way is one way to get things done.
- My way is one way to feel about something or someone.
- There is no "normal"; we are all unique and different.
- My personality is just one among many.
- How can I understand myself and others, and work with humility together with others to get things done?

This is precisely what Paul means in Ephesians 4 v 2, where he calls us to "[bear] with one another in love." Elsewhere, Paul talks about dealing with our own and each other's sin, but "bearing with" someone has to do with differences that are not inherently sinful. It can be tempting to immediately judge someone and make what is essentially a "personality difference" into a "sin difference." But as we change and become more like Jesus, we will find that we view ourselves and others with increasing clarity, charity, and understanding.

UNDERSTANDING YOUR EMOTIONS

One other important aspect of who we are involves our emotions. There is a good bit of overlap between this and our personality.

So what exactly are emotions? This is a hard question to answer. In his ground-breaking 1996 book *Emotional Intelligence*, Dan Goleman says that "all emotions are, in essence, impulses to act, the instant plans for handling life" (*Emotional Intelligence*, p 6).

Try to imagine a day in your life without emotions—simply put, we would not be motivated to do anything! Emotions provide us with a desire to move through life with action.

For our purposes, we will highlight ten standard families of emotions—although there are more blends and variations of emotions than we even have words for! All of these emotions can be expressed in both good and bad ways:

- *Anger:* fury, outrage, resentment, wrath, exasperation, indignation, vexation, acrimony, animosity, annoyance, irritability, hostility, and, perhaps at the extreme, pathological hatred and violence.
- *Sadness:* grief, sorrow, cheerlessness, gloom, melancholy, self-pity, loneliness, dejection, despair, and, when pathological, severe depression.
- *Fear:* anxiety, apprehension, nervousness, concern, consternation, misgiving, wariness, qualm, edginess, dread, fright, terror (phobia and panic).
- *Enjoyment:* happiness, joy, relief, contentment, bliss, delight, amusement, pride, sensual pleasure, thrill, rapture, gratification, satisfaction, euphoria, whimsy, ecstasy (mania).

- *Love:* acceptance, friendliness, trust, kindness, affinity, devotion, adoration, infatuation, *agape*.
- *Surprise:* shock, astonishment, amazement, wonder.
- *Disgust:* contempt, disdain, scorn, abhorrence, aversion, distaste, revulsion.
- *Shame:* guilt, embarrassment, chagrin, remorse, humiliation, regret, mortification, contrition.
- *Inadequacy:* feeling helpless, inferior, powerless, incompetent, useless, inadequate, inept, mediocre, unworthy.
- *Confusion:* feeling distracted, rattled, baffled, anxious, bewildered, mystified, flustered, perplexed, jarred, puzzled, jolted.

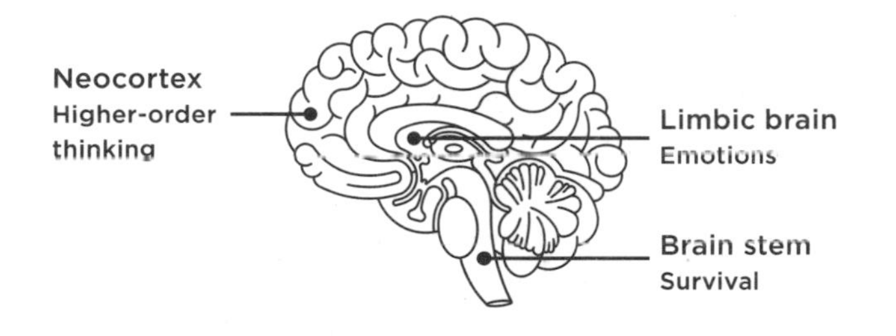

Emotions are formed and generated in the brain, particularly the limbic region—this is the first region after the stem that receives data from your senses. The neocortex is the last area of the brain to receive and process information, where it is analyzed in a more rational way. The goal in emotional regulation is to slow down enough so that the "emotional brain" can work together with the "rational brain" so that we respond appropriately. That's harder than it sounds! Just think about the last time you were hijacked by the limbic region (any time you end up thinking after the fact, "Why in the world did I say or do that?"). In one sense, this entire book is about you slowing things down to look at the various aspects of your life that often go unnoticed. It is like watching scenes from the movies of your life in slow motion!

Remember Mike and Sena at the beginning of the chapter. Their differences are not inherently sinful. Their "comfort level" with certain emotions and the way they express them have been shaped by the kinds of families they grew up in. While it's often the case that "opposites attract," this becomes a source of friction when they fail to remain charitable toward one another's differences and when they don't express their emotions appropriately.

We see in the Bible that there are ways to express emotion that are appropriate and constructive, and ways to express emotion that are inappropriate and destructive. Paul highlights this in Ephesians 4 v 26:

> *"In your anger do not sin": Do not let the sun go down while you are still angry.*

Paul says that a so-called "negative" emotion like anger can be godly (as it's possible to be angry and not sin), and that it can be expressed appropriately.

Not only that: in the second half of the verse he makes a case for emotional intelligence. Paul has Psalm 4 in view:

> *Be angry, and do not sin; ponder in your own hearts on your beds, and be silent. Offer right sacrifices, and put your trust in the* LORD. *(Psalm 4 v 4-5, ESV)*

The psalmist acknowledges that anger can be expressed without sin, but we must slow down and deal with our own heart before the Lord before moving forward. This is a call to self-awareness—that moment when we allow our rational and emotional brains to work in harmony with one another.

We can say from all this that Scripture encourages us to allow time to process our emotions. Whether our emotions are "positive" or "negative," the goal is to express them in ways that are appropriate and constructive. In fact, the Psalms are a window into what it looks like to express positive and negative emotions in godly ways—often it looks like bringing them before God in prayer.

NOT WRONG, JUST DIFFERENT

So what's the point of all of this? Change will look different for each person. It will occur along the contours of one's God-given personality and emotional makeup. Why is it important to state this? Because sometimes we are too quick to go on a sin-hunt in another person's life when what we are dealing with are simple but important differences.

When we think in this way, there are profound implications for all our relationships. Imagine if Joseph and Stuart start to realize that some of their arguments and hurts are due to misunderstanding each other. Imagine that they begin to see differences as simply that—differences that should be appreciated and managed. What if Mike could say to Sena, "Sena, when you process out loud, I feel overwhelmed. I do want to listen but it would help me if you could give me time to process internally and respond before you start speaking again"? What if Sena could say to Mike, "Mike, I love you and care for you. I know that you are an internal processor but when you remain silent for long periods of time, I feel lonely and isolated. I know you don't mean to do that. It would help me if you would simply tell me that you want to talk, but you need some space and time to get your thoughts together"? These kinds of conversations are potential game-changers for your relationships.

WORK IT THROUGH

- Think about the Birkman Map. In which quadrant might you land? Ask a few other people who know you well to tell you what they think. It is possible to have some degree of all the quadrants in your personality. But in general, are you…
    - Extrovert or Introvert?
    - Task or People Oriented?
- Take a moment to think about a few people with whom you interact on a regular basis at work or in your family. Where do you think they fit best?
- Are there areas of your life where you have allowed personality differences to lead to hurtful conflict? If so, what have you read in this chapter that could help you improve these relationships?
- Think about how you express and respond to positive and negative emotions. Is there any connection to how you were raised?
- Think about a few people with whom you interact on a regular basis at work or in your family. How do you think they express and respond to positive and negative emotions?
- Are there relationships where you have allowed differences in the way you express emotions to lead to hurtful conflict? If so, where and how can this chapter help you grow in grace?

While you have a certain predisposition in terms of your personality and emotions, there is still a need to grow in self-awareness, wisdom and Christ-likeness in all of these areas. And the good news is that you can, by the power of the Holy Spirit.

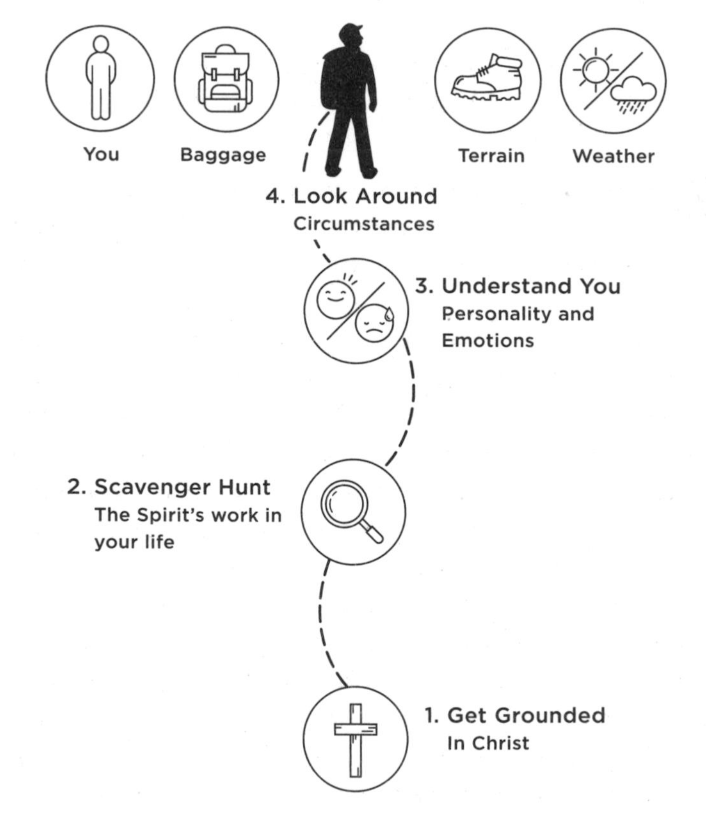

You
Baggage
Terrain
Weather
4. Look Around
Circumstances
3. Understand You
Personality and
Emotions
2. Scavenger Hunt
The Spirit's work in
your life
1. Get Grounded
In Christ

STEP 4
LOOK AROUND

Rightly understand your circumstances.

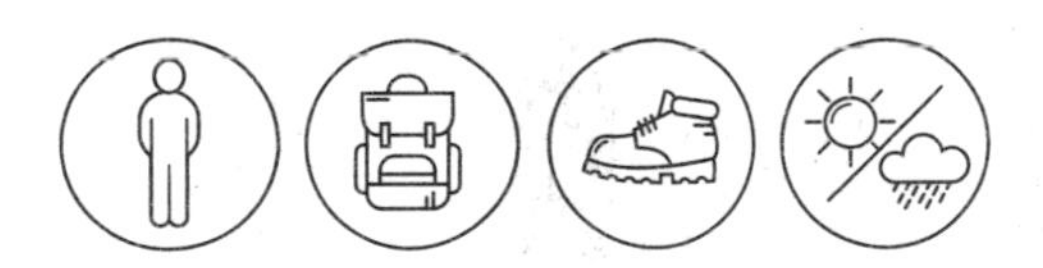

People usually come to me for counseling because they want to change a negative or sinful behavior in their lives. But before I ever start offering any advice, I ask them to tell me their story.

As they do, I become more aware of the things that have shaped them. It is then that I understand why they are struggling in the way they are. Hopefully, if I have listened well, it increases my patience and grace with them. This same thing holds true as you look at your own life. Knowing what has shaped you, for good or for ill, can help you be more patient with yourself as you seek to change.

This fourth step in our journey is often the first thing people tend to focus on, because it is usually the most obvious—what is happening to them. When you get into an argument with a family member, what are you most aware of? Probably the other person and how they are hurting you. At other times the link between our struggle and our circumstances is less clear. For example, if you are feeling anxious, it may require careful thought to put your finger on the precise reason why.

Either way, our circumstances are no small matter, and being appropriately aware of them is a key part of the change process. Why? Because the negative behavior we are seeking to change is a response to our circumstances—and so before we turn our attention to the responses, we need to properly pay attention to the circumstances. That is what we will look at in this chapter.

WHAT DO WE MEAN BY "CIRCUMSTANCES"?

Your circumstances encompass everything outside of your soul or inner person, beginning with your physical body. Psychologists call this the bio/psycho/socio/cultural context in which we live. The Bible uses the words "world" and "body" to capture these categories. God is the creator of the physical world and it is good (Genesis 1 – 2), but the reality of sin in the world means that our lives now include suffering as well as blessing (Genesis 3).

As you imagine standing at a junction, you can think about various aspects of your circumstances in the following categories: you, your baggage, the terrain, and the weather.

1. YOU

This includes your physical body, your brain, and your gender. All three are very important in understanding your personal strengths and struggles.

Your brain: All of us are wired differently. As we saw in the previous chapter, our brains and our unique DNA determine our personalities, but they also predispose us to a host of strengths and weaknesses. Our brains are also impacted by the fall of humanity—we are all broken at some level and exhibit various mental frailties. Recent research in neuroscience is learning a great deal about how the different regions of the brain work and how they interact with each other. The most basic way to think about the brain is in three sections: the stem (survival); the limbic region, including the amygdala (memories, emotions, fight-or-flight responses); and the neocortex (language, abstract thought, consciousness).

Data from our senses travels up our spine and hits these regions in that order. "Neuroplasticity" is a word that describes how pathways are formed in the brain as a result of life experiences and habitual behavior—and that affects the way that we process information. Brain frailties can often be a factor in mental illness. For example, significant depression or anxiety can be a combination of biological and situational factors.

Your body: We have bodies that have strengths and weaknesses. Consider how your body has impacted you in significant ways. Are you tall or short? Were you born with some type of disability or illness? Are you naturally athletic or not? How did that impact you when it came to choosing sides for team sport at school?

Our bodies produce a complex combination of natural chemicals called hormones, and these also impact how we react to our circumstances, including how our brains interpret and respond in real time. Here are a few:

- Serotonin: mood regulation, appetite, memory, sleep, and learning.
- Oxytocin: social behavior, increasing trust and generosity, decreasing fear, and cognitive functions.
- Dopamine: involved in how we think and behave, and our feelings of motivation, reward, and attention.
- Noradrenaline: primes the body for action; elevates the heart rate to increase blood supply to our muscles; triggers the release of glucose from energy stores.
- Cortisol: produced in response to stress to prepare us for a flight-or-fight response.

How these are regulated through exercise, diet, meditation, worship, prayer, and other lifestyle habits is very important.

So caring for our bodies can have a positive influence on the change process.

Your gender: Your gender will have had a significant shaping influence in your life. Take this example: a group of men and a group of women were asked, "When was the last time you were afraid?" The men had a hard time recalling when they last felt unsafe. The women, on the other hand, had no such problem. One woman said, "Last night when I was walking from the grocery store to my car!" While times have changed in many ways, most women still experience life differently than most men. Not only that: research verifies that male and female bodies and hormonal makeup are different. Having children is also a very different experience for men and women. We can see the effects of the fall in the area of gender too. Someone who has suffered from gender dysphoria will have been profoundly affected by that. Have you considered how your gender has shaped the way you respond to life?

2. YOUR BAGGAGE

This captures all the things that have happened to you throughout your life—the blessings and sufferings. Here are several to consider.

Your event and relational history: Can you think of some positive and negative events in your life? How did they impact you? Can you think of some positive and negative people in your life? How did they impact you? For example, Jane grew up in a military family. She moved eight times between the ages of 4 and 18. These moves were significant events that have shaped Jane and affected her relationships.

Our geographical context also shapes us. Jerry grew up in the tornado-prone Midwest. This makes him more anxious when he hears that bad weather is looming. Chloe grew up in a big city. She rarely thinks about bad weather but she is very nervous in traffic!

Your political/cultural/socio-economic context: Consider your political context. Someone growing up in an oppressive dictatorship experiences life very differently than someone who grew up in a democracy. What about your cultural influences? Monica's parents were first-generation immigrants to America, but she was born and educated in the United States. Her cultural context was different from the one that her parents grew up in, and this has shaped her in certain ways. Consider your socio-economic context. Chris grew up in a low-income urban context. Josh, on the other hand, grew up in the suburbs and went to a private school.

The political, cultural, and socio-economic contexts in which we were raised all have a significant impact on how we view life. Can you trace the ways that you have been shaped by your context?

Your religious and moral upbringing: The beliefs that you were taught have shaped the way you respond to life. Sally was raised in a strict, religious home where she was taught to be submissive to all men. Rachel, on the other hand, was told she could grow up to be whatever she wanted to be—she was raised in a very secular home where religion was frowned upon. Bob grew up in a home where he was nurtured with a rich experience of a gracious God who loves him and watches over him. He has fond memories of his mom and dad praying with him and talking to him about the gospel and how it changes people.

What kind of home did you grow up in? Was it religious? Christian? Jewish? Hindu? Buddhist? Muslim? Was it more secular? How did your parents and siblings think about and talk about God? Are your memories positive or negative? Was it legalistic or was there an appropriate emphasis on

God's love and grace? How has this shaped the way you think about the role of faith in your life?

Your race/ethnicity: Whether you are part of the majority or minority culture in a given context will shape the way you experience and respond to life. Mary is black and grew up in a predominantly white neighborhood and school. Enrique is from Puerto Rico but went to college in the UK. André is white and grew up in a very diverse city. Chantelle grew up in a community where she rarely interacted with people who were from different backgrounds. Race and ethnicity impact the way you are perceived and perceive others and your context. How would you self-identify in terms of ethnicity? Did you grow up in the majority culture or a minority culture? What challenges have you experienced? Have you experienced racism, or looked at others through the lens of racist stereotypes?

3. THE TERRAIN

These are the things that are currently happening in your life—your present big-picture situation.

Your age/stage of life: The longer you live, the more life you experience. This can make us wiser and more confident. It can also make us discouraged and bitter. Graham is in his 50s and has recently had heart surgery due to a mild heart attack. Now he is dealing with the fact that he will have to cut back on so many of the sports that he once enjoyed. Judy is in her late 40s and finally feels that she has the confidence she lacked when she was much younger. The experiences of raising three children and growing her career have shaped her into a wise, caring person who can confidently handle challenges with grace. Esther lost her husband five years ago. She also lost a son to a car accident when he was just 30. She doesn't remember things like she used to and gets frustrated when she forgets someone's name.

It tends to be that grief and loss increase the older we become. How old are you? Would you say your confidence has increased or decreased with age? What losses have you experienced? How has that shaped you?

Your work: What is your current job? What types of challenges do you face every morning as you get up? If you are a stay-at-home parent, research has shown that you work the equivalent of two jobs! Are you recently retired? Do you commute to work? What are the people like? Do you report to someone? What are they like? Do you work from home? Your work environment is a large part of your life because you spend a great deal of your waking hours there. What about your current work environment is good, and what is challenging?

Your family: What is your current family situation? Are you single, single again, divorced, married, or married with children? How many children? Who do you live with? Do you live close to extended family or not? What kinds of relationships do you have with your family members? Which relationships are good, and which ones are challenging?

4. THE WEATHER

These are the small micro-moments of daily life, which change throughout any given day and affect our mood. These little moments are often the "triggers" for our responses:

- You had a bad day at work and you come home feeling grumpy and impatient.
- You find an unexpected bill in the mail that you have no resources to pay.
- You discover that someone gossiped about you to a close friend.
- You have just been offered a promotion and will be getting a pay raise.

PUTTING IT TOGETHER

Let's draw what we've seen together with a very simple example. Imagine you get home from work and discover that your roommate hasn't taken the trash out as she promised she would. You feel a wave of annoyance, curse her under your breath, and then send a sarcastic and angry text message. This is an ungodly response.

Consider the circumstances that led up to this response:

- *Weather:* The surface-level trigger for your response is the sight of the overflowing trash can in the corner of the kitchen.
- *Terrain:* Perhaps there's more to it than that. Maybe things are stressful at work for you right now; you've got a big deadline coming up at the end of the week. You've also been caring for a friend who is ill.
- *Baggage:* As we dig a little deeper, consider the sort of home you grew up in. Perhaps yours was a very tidy house. Or maybe your parents put a big emphasis on always keeping your word.
- *Body:* Maybe your sense of smell is very keen. As you walk in the door, all you can smell is rotting trash in the place where you want to cook a nice meal.

It's in response to a culmination of all these circumstances that you respond angrily.

However, in order to change the response, it's important not just to understand the circumstances, but to view them in the right way. Let's start with two wrong ways to view your circumstances.

WRONG WAY # 1

MAKING YOUR CIRCUMSTANCES THE CAUSE FOR YOUR RESPONSE

One wrong way to view this situation would be to blame

your response on that list of factors. Your circumstances are the context for your angry reaction—they are not the cause:

> *When tempted, no one should say, "God is tempting me." For God cannot be tempted by evil, nor does he tempt anyone; but each person is tempted when they are dragged away* ***by their own evil desire*** *and enticed.*
>
> *(James 1 v 13-14)*

James says that sin has its root in what is going on inside the person, not what is going on outside the person. In other words, your circumstances don't make you disobey. They may make it more difficult to obey, but they are the occasion, not the cause, of your response.

WRONG WAY # 2

IGNORING YOUR CIRCUMSTANCES COMPLETELY

Another error runs in the opposite direction. If you minimize your or other people's circumstances, and don't factor them in at all, you will fail to appreciate their influence. You will also miss an opportunity to see how God's grace can help you in the moment (more on that on Step 8). In the previous verse James says this:

> *Blessed is the one who perseveres under trial... (1 v 12)*

James is a pastor writing to his congregation, which has been scattered due to intense persecution (v 1). He never minimizes the challenges of their situation. He acknowledges what they are going through and wants to help them as any caring pastor would. He promises that blessing can come through difficult circumstances. Jesus, too, treats us this way. He does not take our sufferings lightly:

> *For we do not have a high priest who is unable to empathize with our weaknesses, but we have one who has been*

tempted in every way, just as we are—yet he did not sin.
(Hebrews 4 v 15)

Jesus is the perfect high priest—our representative before the Father who empathizes with our situation, and who can deal with our sin. He draws near and remains close to us when we are going through suffering.

It's worth saying that there may be times when your circumstances are so serious that it is appropriate to take immediate action. If you are in an abusive relationship or in danger, please address your circumstances immediately and find safety for you and your dependents.

THE RIGHT WAY

ACKNOWLEDGING YOUR CIRCUMSTANCES

Rather than maximizing or minimizing your circumstances, you must instead see them in their proper perspective. You need to view your circumstances as the context of your current struggle. They are not the cause of your struggle, but they are a significant aspect of your struggle.

This view provides two helpful perspectives. First, it is liberating to know that we are not trapped by our circumstances and that change is possible internally, even if our external situation remains the same. Second, it reminds us of why it is so hard to change—we are complex individuals who often live in challenging situations. Life is hard, but God is with us! Remembering this allows you to forge ahead in a proper direction as you depend upon God's grace.

As we seek to view our circumstances rightly, it also helps to remember that they include both blessing and suffering. First, look for the blessings and humbly thank God. Push against pride and self-sufficiency. Second, look for suffering and be dependent on God, not bitter. Lasting change requires a lot of dependent prayer and patience. God is good, and he will be faithful to walk with you in the good times and in the difficult times.

WORK IT THROUGH

Research has shown that telling your story can be very helpful as you seek to move forward and change. Take a moment and choose a struggle in your life. (If you need help choosing, ask yourself: when was the last time you reacted to your circumstances in a way that was unproductive and ungodly?)

Take that area and consider each of the categories we have been discussing, and then write or tell your "story" in relation to it.

Think about both the blessings and sufferings you have experienced in each of the following categories. Did, or do, any of these aspects of your circumstances play a significant role in this struggle?

- *You*
  Your brain
  Your physical body
  Your gender
- *Baggage*
  Your event and relational history
  Your political/cultural/socio-economic context
  Your religious and moral context
  Your ethnicity
- *Terrain*
  Your age and season of life
  Your current work
  Your current family relationships
- *Weather*
  Current smaller issues that are your typical triggers associated with this struggle.

GIVE THANKS AND GRIEVE

When you're finished, take time to give thanks for the strengths and blessings in each area. Also, pay attention to ways you have suffered. Know that grieving is an important part of growing through difficulties. This will also enable you to pay attention to the areas where you are more vulnerable. This will increase your patience as you pursue lasting change.

Consider doing this exercise with a friend who is struggling in an area of their lives. If you do this, err on the side of listening, asking helpful questions, and just understanding, instead of giving unsolicited advice. Imagine how understanding their story and context will enable you to have more empathy as you walk with them through temptation or suffering.

Your circumstances shape you but they do not define you—what defines you is that you are in a relationship with a God who loves you. He is a living Savior and King and he has placed his Spirit within you. That means that however tough your circumstances are, they cannot keep you stuck—it is possible to respond to them with increasing love, patience, grace, and joy. Indeed, that is what he calls you to, and that is what he has equipped you for.

We'll see how to go about changing your responses in the next chapter. But for now, remember that although circumstances may be stacked against you, God is for you.

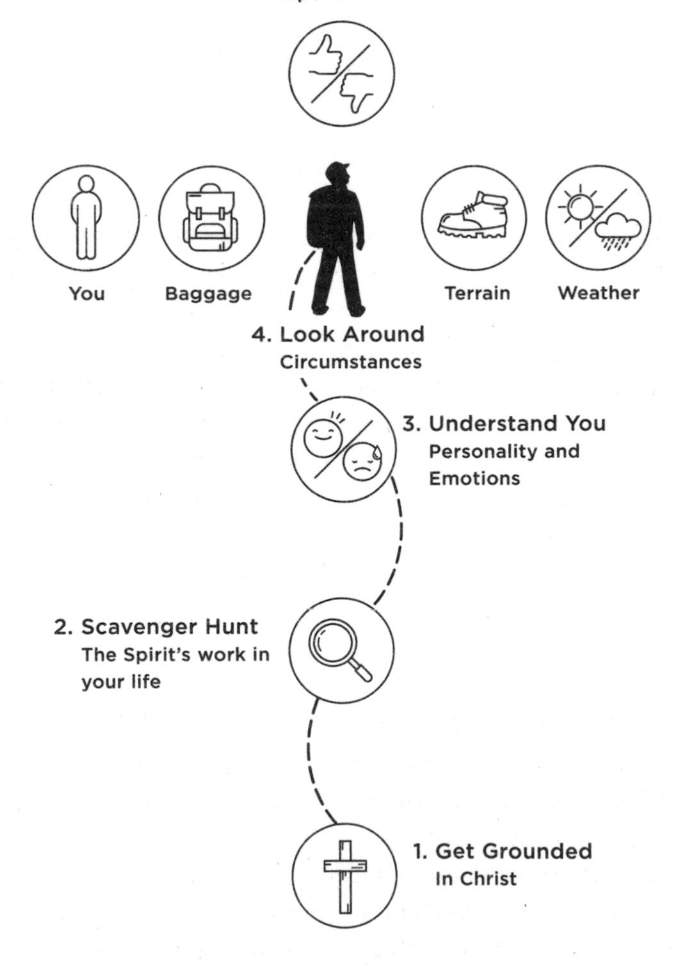
5. Gauge Your Reactions
How did you respond?
You
Baggage
Terrain
Weather
4. Look Around
Circumstances
3. Understand You
Personality and Emotions
2. Scavenger Hunt
The Spirit's work in your life
1. Get Grounded
In Christ

STEP 5
GAUGE YOUR REACTIONS

Pay attention to your responses.

The other day, I was driving my car to my office and I noticed that a warning light appeared on the dashboard. It was a signal that there was a problem in the engine.

Your responses to your circumstances are like that warning light. When you respond to life in ways that are unwise and potentially sinful, that means that there is something wrong at a deeper level: there is a problem in your heart. In the same way that the warning light on the dash points to a deeper problem, your behavior is a warning light that you must see before you can address the deeper issues. So Step 5 in our journey of change is to think about our responses to life's circumstances.

THE JOURNEY SO FAR

In this chapter, we take our first pivot to look inward in a "critical" way. But before we do, remember where we have traveled so far.

You are in Christ and secure in his love because of his life, death and resurrection (Step 1). The Holy Spirit is already at work in you (Step 2). You've paused to consider your personality and emotions, to gauge what change will look like, given your natural strengths and weaknesses

(Step 3). You've begun to pay attention to your circumstances—body, baggage, terrain and weather—without maximizing or minimizing them (Step 4).

Now, as you stand at the junction, the question is: how will you respond to your circumstances? When the kids are disrespecting you, or a big deadline is making you anxious, or you're tempted to click the link to a pornographic website—how will you react? Will you go left—responding in a way that is ungodly or unhelpful—or right—responding in a way that is godly and productive?

If you've read this far, it's because you're stuck taking the left route. So let's explore how that looks exactly.

A GENTLE WARNING

Since Step 5 requires you to focus on your unwise and/or ungodly responses to your situation, you need a gentle warning in order to avoid proceeding in one of the following ways.

The first is to *live in denial*, by minimizing or even denying your responses. Typically, this type of person tends to stay busy to avoid looking at themselves or their behavior.

The second is to turn inward and *live in shame* under a cloud of guilt. If you go in this direction, you are sure to lapse into a morbid introspection that will certainly rob you of any joy or desire to change.

Neither of these mindsets are helpful, nor does Scripture invite us to look at our responses in this way. The language of the gospel is that you are free to struggle; you are not struggling so that you can be free. God accepts you because Jesus has paid for your guilt and shame. He doesn't tell you to work on your guilt and shame so that maybe he will accept you. So slow down and take a moment to thank God for his grace. Take a few deep breaths as you meditate on God's love, which he has so richly lavished on you

(1 John 3 v 1). You are living under a monsoon of God's love for you in Christ.

As you do this, it will help you to evaluate your responses in a way that is encouraging rather than discouraging.

THE LIFE THAT JESUS LOOKS FOR

So what are the responses to life that God desires? What are we aiming for? On one level, it's pretty simple. Jesus summarizes it in one word: "Love."

> *"Love the Lord your God with all your heart and with all your soul and with all your mind." This is the first and greatest commandment. And the second is like it: "Love your neighbor as yourself." All of the Law and the Prophets hang on these two commandments. (Matthew 22 v 37-40)*

Notice that the order begins with a new relationship with God that shows itself in new relationships with the people around us. There is a vertical and a horizontal dimension.

In other parts of Scripture, we find more detailed descriptions of the responses that God desires from his people. For example, Galatians 5 lists the acts (or responses) of "the flesh" (v 19-21) and then the acts of "the Spirit" (v 22-26). These two lists serve as a sort of "What not to do" and "What to do" of the Christian life. It is important to remember that these are not arbitrary rules being imposed on you, but loving guidelines that are good for you and enable you to show your gratitude to God for his grace.

"The flesh"—or "the old nature"—is Paul's shorthand for the remaining presence of sin in our lives. While Christians are no longer slaves to sin (v 1), it still has a powerful pull in our lives. That is why the Bible talks about the Christian life as a fight: because at the same time as feeling sin's pull, we "live by the Spirit" (v 25)—we are spiritually alive to God and his presence and power are in us by the

Holy Spirit. Sometimes this is called the "new nature" or "new heart."

While it is new, it is not yet perfect! Think of it this way. Before we became Christians, "left" was our natural route. Now we live by the Spirit, we can choose "right." And one day in eternity, we'll always walk "right," because the left path of sin will be no more.

But until then, we keep battling. So let's take a look at those lists.

UNWISE RESPONSES:
LIFE ACCORDING TO THE SINFUL NATURE

> *The acts of the [sinful nature] are obvious: sexual immorality, impurity and debauchery; idolatry and witchcraft; hatred, discord, jealousy, fits of rage, selfish ambition, dissensions, factions and envy; drunkenness, orgies, and the like. I warn you, as I did before, that those who live like this will not inherit the kingdom of God.* (v 19-21)

- *False worship.* "Idolatry and witchcraft": this includes any form of worship that is not directed toward the Christian God: Father, Son, and Spirit. We are prone to worship (essentially, "give worth to") many other things instead—from our relationships to our reputation. Notice that false worship leads to a host of behaviors that are ungodly.
- *A lack of self-control over bodily pleasures like sex, food, and drink.* "Sexual immorality, impurity and debauchery … drunkenness, orgies, and the like": this includes any sexual activity between unmarried people (real or imagined), unnatural sexual practices and relationships, and uncontrolled sexuality.
- *Destructive attitudes:* "Hatred … jealousy … selfish ambition … envy."

- *Destructive results of destructive attitudes toward others:* "Discord … fits of rage … dissensions, factions."

Paul says that anyone who practices these things without any repentance is not a Christian—they "will not inherit the kingdom of God" (v 21). But remember, this list is being written to a group of believers. That must mean that Christians can be tempted to live in these ways. Because we are not made completely perfect when we become Christians, we will see ongoing warfare and struggle in these areas; and in some areas more than others, due to the life-shaping experiences that we discussed on Step 4. One Christian may be more prone to struggle in the area of sexual purity, while another may be more prone to struggle with an attitude of envy.

Nonetheless, this first list highlights those things that are contrary to change.

WISE RESPONSES:
LIFE ACCORDING TO THE SPIRIT

In the next list, Paul shows us the character qualities that should be developing in us as a consequence of our new relationship with God:

> *But the fruit of the Spirit is love, joy, peace, forbearance, kindness, goodness, faithfulness, gentleness and self-control. Against such things there is no law. Those who belong to Christ Jesus have crucified the [sinful nature] with its passions and desires. Since we live by the Spirit, let us keep in step with the Spirit.* (v 22-25)

Paul lists three sets of three qualities, which encompass all of life: your relationship with God, others, and yourself. Notice how they are contrasted to the list of sinful responses listed above.

- *Your attitude toward God: true worship*
  Love: For God in light of all he has done for you in Christ.
  Joy: A delight in God for who he is, not just for what he has to offer.
  Peace: You have peace with God, and you have confidence and rest in his wisdom and sovereignty.
- *Your attitude toward others: love for others*
  Forbearance: Patience with others when they sin against you or persecute you.
  Kindness: A general disposition of humility and encouragement toward others.
  Goodness: Showing God's love to others in word and deed.
- *Your personal integrity: self-control*
  Faithfulness: To be utterly reliable and true to your word.
  Gentleness: Being humble in your own self-assessment rather than self-righteous.
  Self-control: Expressed in faithfulness and gentleness, rather than being carried along by your impulses.

These two lists could not be any more different! And God desires for every one of his children to grow this fruit, because these godly responses reflect his own character. This is precisely what the Holy Spirit wants to do in your life. Amazing! And as you look down that list, isn't that what you want too? Wouldn't it be wonderful to always live like that? Scripture paints a picture of godly living in order to spur you on to change. You can find similar comparisons between the "old" lifestyle and the "new" lifestyle in passages like Colossians 3 v 5-17, Ephesians 4 v 17-32 and James 3 v 13-18.

These lists should lead us to ask questions about our behavior: How am I responding to life's circumstances?

Where do I see myself displaying these character qualities? Where do I see growth that I can be grateful to God for? What are the areas where I need to grow?

"IF ... THEN" VERSUS "SINCE ... THEN" THINKING

Greg had been struggling with moodiness for several years. He was edgy and angry most of the time. When I first met him, he complained about not being happy anymore with his work. His colleagues never knew what kind of mood he would be in from day to day. His marriage was not doing well either. He and his wife were living parallel lives. They had gotten to the point where they rarely interacted with each other unless it was over a scheduling issue with their children or church. Greg also told me that he just didn't feel connected to God in any way. Going to church felt like going through the motions. The sermons and songs were completely irrelevant to his day-to-day struggles at work and home. Nothing ever seemed to be helpful.

As Greg talked about his personal moods, he was quick to point fingers at his job, wife, kids, and church. In other words, Greg was making his circumstances his primary focus. He thought that the way to change was to change the things around him. This is "If ... then" thinking. Essentially: *If my circumstances were different, then I would be different.*

Greg reasoned that if his work was more enjoyable, then he would be better. If his wife would pay him some attention, then he would be kinder. If his children would be more respectful, then he would be more encouraging. Greg's "If ... then" list was growing by the month. Whenever a new external pressure would arise, it would be added to the list: finances, an upset customer, a picky neighbor, a bad driver, or even the government! It was obvious that Greg was in a very bad place. He couldn't understand why everyone seemed to avoid him!

Do you see how easy it is to focus on our circumstances and not our own responses to our circumstances?

But imagine what would happen if Greg moved from "If ... then" thinking to "Since ... then" thinking. That is precisely what we see in Galatians 5 v 25: "Since we live by the Spirit, [then] let us keep in step with the Spirit." "If ... then" thinking focuses on changing your circumstances. "Since ... then" thinking focuses on changing your perspective! It fixes your eyes on who God has made you, not where he has placed you. *Since* you have been given a new nature, *then* you can look at your reactions to your circumstances, honestly face your ungodly responses, and be open to the possibility of repentance and change. Our "if ... then" must become "since ... then" thinking if we are going to achieve lasting change.

WORK IT THROUGH

Let's get very practical. Remember, Scripture calls us to pay attention to the way we are responding to life with prayerful self-examination (Psalm 4 v 4). To help you, I have adapted a process from *The Anxiety and Worry Workbook* by David Clark and Aaron T. Beck, which can be applied to any issue you are seeking to address. At this stage we're looking at our responses and asking, "What?". In the next chapter we will begin to ask, "Why?"

Pick a recent situation where you responded in an ungodly way. Use the following framework to write down your answers and reflections.

PHYSICAL SENSATIONS AND EMOTIONS

Identifying the bodily sensations and emotions we experience in response to life can be very helpful. Remember, all emotions can be expressed in godly and ungodly ways. For now, we are focusing in on problem emotions.

- Over the course of a week, pay attention to your emotions and try to identify what triggered your response. The aim is to determine if there are recurring patterns of similar circumstances and responses. Use the list on pages 48-49 to help you identify what you are feeling.
- While you do this, rate the intensity of your struggle on a scale of 1-10.
- Describe the physical sensations associated with your emotions. This may involve increased heart rate, muscle tension, chest discomfort, body temperature, chill or hot flashes, and so on.
- Do your initial emotional and physical sensations provoke a further emotional response? For example, do you find yourself experiencing guilt and shame as a result of your anger? This can further complicate the ability to address your behaviors and experience change.

THINKING PATTERNS

We all are trying to make sense of what is happening around us. What negative thinking patterns do you see?

- Catastrophizing: "I am going to do the same old thing."
- Jumping to conclusions: "Murphy's Law—if something can go wrong, it probably will."
- Tunnel vision: "I am only able to think about my typical way of responding."
- Nearsightedness: "I am stuck in the moment and can't see past it."
- Emotional reasoning: "I am going to lose it and really embarrass myself."
- All-or-nothing thinking: "Either this is going to be great or terrible."
- What other thinking patterns can you identify?

BELIEFS

This aspect of your response is tied to deeper issues that we will consider later. In the moment, as best as you can, identify false beliefs that are happening at a deeper level.

- *What do you believe about the situation?* "Here I am again." "This person is out to get me." "Life is too much to bear."
- *What do you believe about yourself?* "I am all alone." "I deserve what I want." "I am better than you." "I am worthless."
- *What do you believe about God?* "God is nowhere to be found." "God is not for me." "God is punishing me."
- *What do you believe about other people?* "Other people are a hassle." "They are trying to do me wrong." "If I can't have your approval, I will be undone." "You owe me respect."
- *What do you believe will help you avoid what you don't want to happen?* "If I just remain silent, no one will come after me." "I need to tell that person just what I am thinking." "I should avoid that event so I don't embarrass myself."

SPECIFIC BEHAVIORS

These are the visible responses and ways by which you seek to manage/control your circumstances.

- Avoidance behaviors: You check out either by physically avoiding the situation or seeking comfort in a usually addictive behavior like eating, watching TV, using some chemical substance, and so on (see final point).
- Controlling behaviors: These usually involve trying to exert your power in a situation to overcome any obstacles. Anger is very common, but so are obsessive behaviors.
- Addictive behaviors: The main theme in these behaviors is an attempt to minimize pain and maximize pleasure.

> There are many addictive behaviors that don't involve a substance. Shopping or cleaning your house could be an addictive behavior.

Take a moment to see how your unproductive and/or ungodly responses to your circumstances are potentially making things worse. This is a bit tricky because these behaviors can give you the illusion that they are helping. Try to look further down the path to see how they might become problematic in the long run. These responses will only complicate your struggles and add more layers to the problem, which will make it harder to change.

As you can see, this is a fairly comprehensive overview of your responses—and it will take time to process! You might want to linger for a while on this step, prayerfully reflecting on your responses at the end of each day in order to really understand them. This step in the change process is critical if you are going to see long-lasting change. These responses have likely become so natural that you don't even recognize them. You may want to choose another issue in your life and walk through these various categories to see if you discern any recurring patterns. Don't be surprised if you do!

NEVER REJECTED

Remember, if you are not careful, this step could backfire on you. If dwelling on this step discourages you, go back to Steps 1, 2, 3, and 4! Keep these two truths in mind:

> *Therefore, there is now no condemnation for those who are in Christ Jesus, because through Christ Jesus the law of the Spirit who gives life has set you free from the law of sin and death.* (Romans 8 v 1-2)

> *[Be] confident of this, that he who began a good work in you will carry it on to completion until the day of Christ Jesus.*
> *(Philippians 1 v 6)*

Considering our responses is crucial if we are going to make progress in the change process. While it may not be fun, it is necessary.

But don't lose heart. The Bible constantly holds out hope for people like you and me who struggle on a daily basis to love God and neighbor. So as you look at your responses, remember that however much you dislike what you see—however ugly your thoughts and behavior seem—if you are in Christ, then God does not and will not reject you. If you're repenting of your sin and trusting Christ to forgive you, then he does not and will not condemn you. Instead, he draws you close, fills you with his Spirit, and empowers you to change.

6. Look Underneath
Why did you respond like that?

5. Gauge Your Reactions
How did you respond?

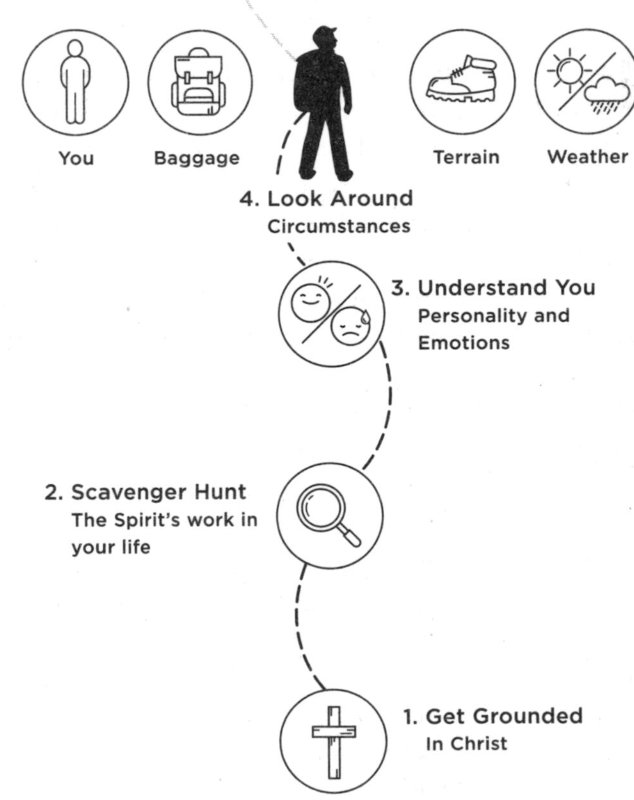

STEP 6
LOOK UNDERNEATH

Ask the "why" and "what" questions.

Have you ever been in a situation like this: you're in a heated conversation with someone, and it is just the two of you in a room. In the middle of the argument, your cell phone rings or someone else enters the room—and in an instant, you change from being agitated and angry to being calm and sensitive! Why are we able to change so quickly when there's an audience? The answer to that question reveals something critical to the change process.

ROOTS, SHOOTS, AND ENGINES

In the previous chapter, we discussed how our responses to life's circumstances are like the warning light on the dashboard of a car: they show us that something is wrong. In this chapter, we want to get under the hood and see the engine that is driving the behavior. We want to find out why we are responding in a specific way.

Various words are used in the Bible to talk about the human "engine": heart, soul, mind, spirit, and strength. Essentially, all these terms refer to the inner person.

God has created you with a body and a soul. You have both an outer person and an inner person. And, according to James 3 v 9-12, the two are intimately linked:

With the tongue we praise our Lord and Father, and with it we curse human beings, who have been made in God's likeness. Out of the same mouth come praise and cursing. My brothers and sisters, this should not be. Can both fresh water and salt water flow from the same spring? My brothers and sisters, can a fig tree bear olives, or a grapevine bear figs? Neither can a salt spring produce fresh water.

Do you see what James is saying? Your responses to life (in this case, your speech) are ultimately driven by what kind of root system is underneath the surface. If your roots are fig roots, you will bear figs. If your root system is that of a grapevine, you will bear grapes. The roots determine the fruit. Similarly, the type of water at the source of a spring will determine what kind of water you have downstream.

It all comes down to the inner person. As you can see, the Bible has a vivid way of talking about human behavior and motivation.

YOUR ULTIMATE DEFINITION

As in the last chapter, it's worth saying again that the more we look inward, the more we must keep the grace of the gospel central. Your ultimate identity is not found in a specific struggle with some temptation or sinful behavior, nor is it located in some form of suffering you may have experienced. If you are in Christ, you belong to God and you are deeply loved by him. As you see places in your life that are problematic, don't let guilt and shame twist the way you see yourself. Get some perspective, and look back at what you have learned about yourself and what is ultimately true of you. No sin or experience of suffering can define who you are! You are defined by who Jesus is and what he has done for you in his life, death, and resurrection. Remember, you are "in" Christ: you are viewed and treated by God in the same way that Jesus is viewed and treated by the Father (John 17 v 23). In addition, don't forget to factor in all the shaping influences—the blessings and challenges—we considered in chapter 3. This will help you to avoid the debilitating aspects of guilt and shame.

ASKING THE "WHY" AND "WHAT" QUESTIONS

If lasting change is going to happen, you must begin to ask "why?" and "what?" questions. Here is what they sound like:

- Why do I do the things I do?
- What motivates me to do the things I do, either good or bad, helpful or unhelpful?

We've seen in previous chapters that Christians are called to Spirit-led self-awareness. This self-examination includes seeing Christ, his work in us, our circumstances, and our behaviors; but it also goes deeper. We must seek to grow in an awareness of what drives that behavior. Paul encourages this kind of insight in Philippians 2 v 3:

> *Do nothing out of selfish ambition or vain conceit. Rather, in humility value others above yourselves.*

Selfish ambition and vain conceit are attitudes of the inner person that express themselves in behaviors that put ourselves first, instead of seeking the wellbeing of others. In verse 5 Paul goes on to say that we should "have the same mindset as Christ Jesus." Why? Because our behaviors grow out of fundamental attitudes. This is Paul's way of talking about the deeper motivations that drive responses.

Paul shows us the other side of the coin in Romans 1 v 25, where he describes the inner disposition of the non-believer:

> *They exchanged the truth about God for a lie, and worshiped and served created things rather than the Creator.*

Human beings are fundamentally worshipers. The word "worship" means to give worth to something: to honor something or to revolve your life around it. Paul says that the tendency for all human beings is to find something (or many things) in the created world and revolve their life around that, rather than around the only one who rightly deserves our worship: the true Creator God. It is this fundamental attitude or disposition of the inner person that will express itself in specific behaviors. Here's how that might look:

- If I worship and revolve my life around being in control, I will likely be easily agitated and angry when things feel out of my control. But if I find my identity and confidence in who I am in Christ, I will hold my plans more loosely. I'll show increasing patience towards others as I entrust myself to the One who is completely in control.
- If I worship and revolve my life around being liked, I will likely fear confrontation and avoid it at all costs. But if I find my identity and confidence in who I am in Christ, I will be more open to having honest and helpful conversations with people with whom I disagree.
- If I worship and revolve my life around comfort, I will likely try to avoid pain or inconvenience, and may be prone to finding comfort in things that numb me to life's hardships. But if I find my identity and confidence in who I am in Christ, I will be more able to accept hardship, because Jesus comforts me with his Spirit.

Jesus confirms this perspective most clearly in Luke 6:

> *No good tree bears bad fruit, nor does a bad tree bear good fruit. Each tree is recognized by its own fruit. People do not pick figs from thornbushes, or grapes from briers. A good man brings good things out of the good stored up in*

> *his heart, and an evil man brings evil things out of the evil stored up in his heart. For the mouth speaks what the heart is full of.* *(v 43-45)*

Jesus uses a similar metaphor to James to talk about human behavior. The whole of Scripture paints a broad picture of what ultimately drives our behaviors: it is a fundamental orientation of one's inner person.

WHAT'S UNDER THE HOOD?

Why is all this so important? Imagine again that you are driving down the road and you notice that the temperature gauge on your dashboard is running high. You know this is not good. So you stop at a mechanic, and he assures you that he can fix the problem. He proceeds to break the glass over the gauge, move the needle back to where it should be, and then tape it down to stop it from moving anymore!

You would probably think that the mechanic was out of his mind. The gauge is not the problem—the problem is under the hood in the engine! A good mechanic would diagnose what was causing the engine to run hot by a process of elimination—is it a bad water-pump, a broken belt, a hole in the radiator, low oil, a busted hose, or something else? The mechanic would need to get under the hood and diagnose the problem in order to fix it. Only then would the temperature gauge return to its normal and appropriate level.

The same can be said of humans and their behavior. If you see good or bad behavior (like the gauge), it is revealing what is going on in that person's heart (under the hood). Proper diagnosis can then lead to proper treatment of the problem.

One note of caution: it takes a professional to diagnose what is wrong with a car engine, and even then it is not always easy. And people are much more complex than car engines. Therefore, it is important to move carefully and wisely when asking the "why?" and "what?" questions. You want to avoid becoming simplistic when assessing motivational drives in yourself or others. You certainly don't want to assume that you have such clear discernment that you have the right to go on a sin-hunt in someone else's life. There could be devastating consequences if you are not careful, wise, and loving in how you help others grow in self-awareness. And when it comes to diagnosing your own heart, do ask for help if you need it, from a pastor, counselor, or mature Christian friend. This is not a sign of weakness but of strength!

THE TOOLS OF THE TRADE

So how do we begin the process of diagnosis? How do we begin to determine why we respond in unproductive and ungodly ways to our circumstances? Like a mechanic, we need the right tools. In the rest of this chapter we'll practice using three tools (or questions) that help us see more clearly what we were living for in a particular moment.

In the moments when you choose the left fork at the junction, these are the questions you need to ask yourself:

- Why did I do what I did?
- What did I *want* in the moment that I was *not* getting?
- What did I *not want* in the moment that I *was* getting?

These three simple questions will open a window into what you tend to live for and what drives your responses to your circumstances. Let's consider three common struggles and apply what we have learned in this chapter. Keep in mind that these are very simple examples. In real life, our struggles may be more or less complex depending on the shaping influences that we read about on Step 4. Also keep in mind that we are not addressing how God's grace changes us at this point. We will look at that in the following chapters.

ANGER

Let's reflect on the example at the beginning of this chapter of two people arguing and then suddenly stopping when one of their cell phones rings.

Imagine you are arguing with another person.

- *Why?* Because they are getting in the way of something you want and giving you something you don't want.
- *What do you want/not want?* You might want comfort, respect, affirmation, acceptance, and/or peace, but you are getting disrespect, disagreement, rejection, or disruption. As a result, you are irritated and frustrated with the person you are speaking with.

You change immediately when your cell phone rings and you become very polite.

- *Why?* Because you are concerned about your reputation.
- *What do you want/not want?* You want to be viewed as a kind person by the person who called you, so you change your tone of voice. You instinctively want to keep your reputation intact. You don't want them to think poorly of you.

As you can see, the driving motivation underneath your anger before the phone call is getting your way. That quickly shifts when the phone rings, and suddenly your reputation and what others think of you is most important to you. This is how the desires "under the hood" cause us to act in certain ways.

ANXIETY

Consider the last time you struggled with fear, worry, or anxiety. Maybe you had a speech that you had to present to a large group. Perhaps you were concerned about financ-es or a relationship. There are all kinds of things that can cause us to struggle with anxiety.

Let's imagine that, as a supervisor, you need to have an honest conversation with a co-worker who has been very difficult lately. The night before, you can't stop thinking about the conversation you must have the next day. Moments before the appointment, you can feel your heart start to race and your palms get sweaty. You even feel your neck and face getting a little flushed.

- *Why?* You are concerned that this co-worker may not like you after the conversation/confrontation.
- *What do you want/not want?* You want to be liked. You want people to say nice things about you and have a positive opinion of you. You don't want to experience rejection.

During the appointment, you duck the conversation; you choose not to say anything and keep things pleasant.

- *Why?* You can't bear the idea that someone would get upset and reject you.
- *What do you want/not want?* You want to be liked. Being disliked feels like being out of control. It feels too much like being rejected or even abandoned. You can't stand that feeling. Perhaps this derives from an incident or incidents in your past.

In this scenario, the driving motivation is to avoid rejection or abandonment and to maintain the peace. While this may work for a while, you find that you can't always control what people think of you, so the whole cycle of fear and anxiety continues and the problems with your co-worker do not get resolved.

ADDICTION

Consider the last time you were hurting and you decided to find comfort and relief in some experience. Perhaps you experienced a failure and you decided to numb the pain of your failure by drinking to the point of drunkenness. Or perhaps you just drank enough to help you calm down and feel better. Of course, your "substance" of choice could be anything: ice-cream, potato chips, cleaning your house, watching TV, putting on some music and tuning out. Each of these things can be good in their own way, but for some of us, one or more of these may become our "go to" way of escape. This is revealed by the fact that we overindulge.

Imagine that the past several months have been hard. Work has been non-stop, your teenage son is failing his senior-year algebra class, finances are tight, and you and your spouse have been distant, not getting along. With all of this going on, you have found yourself in a pattern of having several mixed drinks most evenings while you surf the internet and listen to music on your headphones. You check out of engaging with the family and stay up late.

- *Why?* Life is hard and you feel pressed on all sides. Nothing seems to be going right. You feel raw and alone.
- *What do you want/not want?* You want something to take the edge off reality. You are worn down and you want some comfort. You desire time out from the daily grind—you feel that you owe yourself some downtime. You don't want to experience any more pain or discomfort.

In all three of these scenarios, if something isn't done, there will be consequences. In the words of the passage of Galatians that we looked at in the last chapter, if you continue to give in to the desires of the flesh, then there will be consequences: what you sow you will reap (Galatians 6 v 7).

If the pattern of this final example continues, it could become a full-on addictive behavior. The more you drink, the more it has an impact on your brain. Over time, as the reward centers of your brain respond to the chemical high of your alcohol and internet binges, this connects with the memory center of your brain. Each morning you get up to face another day, and your memory center kicks in and recalls the good feeling you had last night (even if you are hung over). So you start to plan for 7 p.m. all over again.

What started as an innocuous habit soon becomes an addiction. Everyone but you can see it. You start to revolve your life around your beverage of choice. It becomes a ritual that is so ingrained in your daily routine that you manipulate others when they confront you, or you use them to get what you want. As a result, things with your spouse and kids get worse, and eventually your work is suffering from your addictive behavior.

WHERE'S YOUR TREASURE?

Those three problems—anger, anxiety, and addiction—are as old as humanity itself. One Christian psychiatrist has put it this way:

> *To be alive is to be addicted, and to be alive and addicted is to stand in need of grace.*
>
> *(Gerald May, Addiction and Grace, p 16)*

The word "addicted" in that quote could just as easily be replaced with "angry" or "anxious". Individuals may be more vulnerable to one or the other—possibly due to biology and/or significant life-shaping circumstances. Still, when we peel back all the layers, the deeper motivational drive is always found just where Scripture says it is: in the human heart. Jesus said this in Matthew 6 v 21:

> *Where your treasure is, there your heart will be also.*

In other words, whatever you live for, desire, worship, serve, make central to your existence, or revolve your life around… this will be what captivates your heart, and what will in turn determine how you respond to life as you experience it. One of the most important steps in getting unstuck is seeing what that is, or those things are. We are usually driven by a complex web of motives, but it helps to start by thinking of them one at a time.

Did any of the wants and desires, fears and longings that we discussed in this chapter strike close to home? If not, what else might be going on in your heart? What do you live for, functionally? What do you naturally think about when your mind is left to wander? Success, pleasure, acceptance, status, power, control, wealth, comfort? These are key indications of where your "treasure" is.

WORK IT THROUGH

Take a recent situation and describe what was going on and how you responded in an unproductive and ungodly way. Now begin to ask the "why?" and "what?" questions.

- Why did I do what I did?
- What did I want that I was not getting?
- What did I not want that I was getting?

Chances are, as you do this in a variety of areas in your life, you will probably see particular themes that show up in many other areas of your life. As a Christian, seeing these patterns can help you engage in meaningful repentance and help you start to change. Remember that whatever our struggle, all of us stand in need of need of grace. And whatever our struggle, God has and will continue to "give us more grace" through Christ (James 4 v 6).

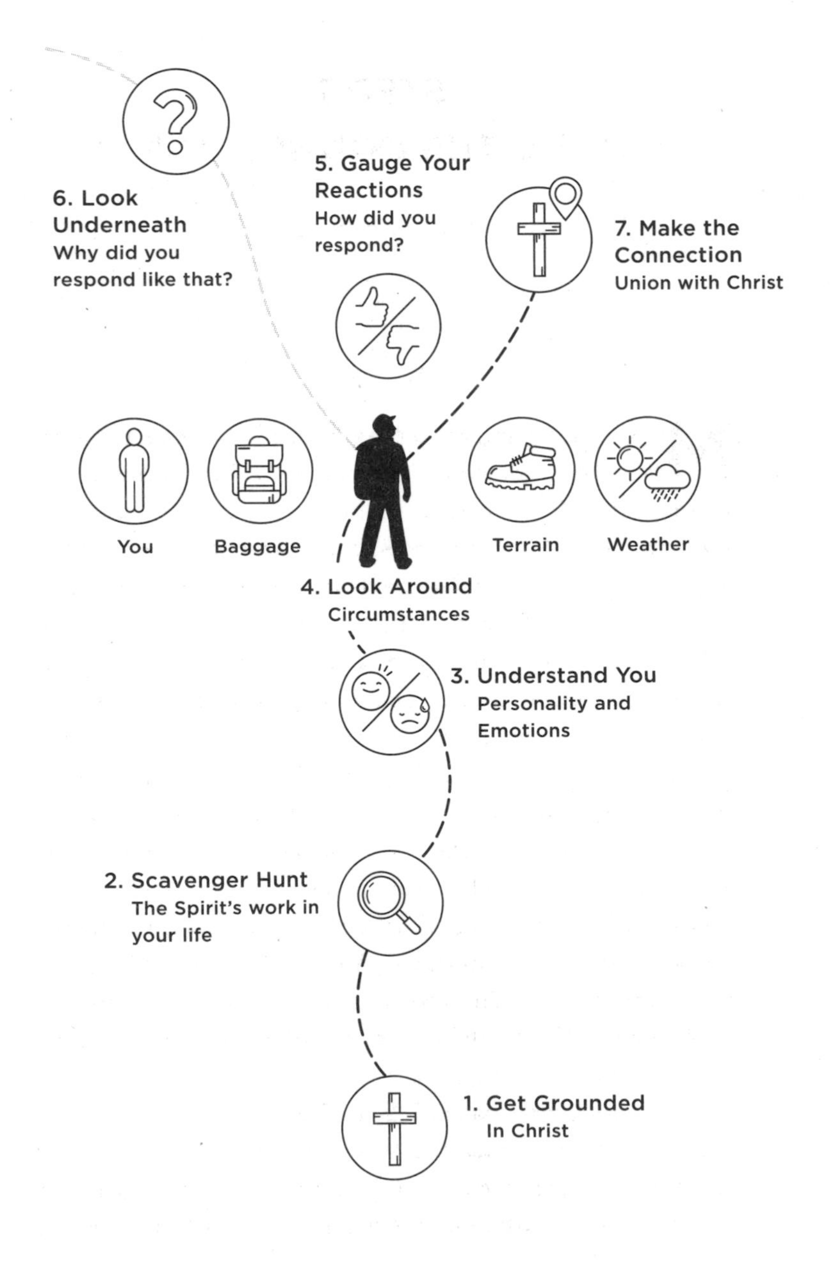
6. Look Underneath
Why did you respond like that?
5. Gauge Your Reactions
How did you respond?
7. Make the Connection
Union with Christ
You
Baggage
Terrain
Weather
4. Look Around
Circumstances
3. Understand You
Personality and Emotions
2. Scavenger Hunt
The Spirit's work in your life
1. Get Grounded
In Christ

STEP 7
MAKE THE CONNECTION

Remember that you are united to Christ.

My wife, Barbara, and I have always had a love for turning old, outdated houses into something entirely new. In the nearly 30 years that we have been married, we have lived in four different homes, three of which were "fixer uppers". You can probably guess that the fourth was not!

The process of renovating a home is exhilarating and exhausting at the same time. The most challenging project was the third home. The foundation and the structure were in good shape, but it was in desperate need of an entire makeover. Walls needed to be torn down, plumbing had to be completely redone, electrical wires and boxes had to be upgraded. What made things worse was that we did all the renovation while we lived in the house with four young children. We even went without a kitchen for three months. All six of us would gather in our small bedroom and eat meals from a crockpot or order pizzas. We made a promise to one another that we would never do that again!

It was downright painful! But when it was all done, that home was a great pleasure to enjoy, and we loved entertaining and raising our family there. Once we were on the other side of the deconstruction and could live in the newly reconstructed rooms, it put the pain of the process in perspective.

The point is this: when you are engaged in the process of change, it usually requires a lot of demolition and deconstruction long before you can see the new growth emerge. Old habits, patterns, and beliefs must be entirely reworked. Walls of denial must come down. The heart and head need rewiring. And all this while we are "living" there! C.S. Lewis captures this well in his book *Mere Christianity*:

> *Imagine yourself as a living house. God comes in to rebuild that house. At first, perhaps, you can understand what he is doing. He is getting the drains right and stopping the leaks in the roof and so on; you knew that those jobs needed doing and so you are not surprised. But presently he starts knocking the house about in a way that hurts abominably and does not seem to make any sense. What on earth is he up to? The explanation is that he is building quite a different house from the one you thought of—throwing out a new wing here, putting on an extra floor there, running up towers, making courtyards. You thought you were being made into a decent little cottage: but he is building a palace. He intends to come and live in it himself.*
>
> *(C.S. Lewis, Mere Christianity, p 160)*

By this stage in our journey, you might be feeling bruised and discouraged at the rate of progress you have made. While it may be tempting to lose hope, know that Christ is already working in you and will continue to work in you. Don't lose sight of the end goal—becoming like Christ:

> *Dear friends, now we are children of God, and what we will be has not yet been made known. Be we know that when Christ appears, we shall be like him, for we shall see*

> *him as he is. All who have this hope in him purify themselves, just as he is pure.* (1 John 3 v 2-3)

One day we will meet Christ face to face, and the renovation work on our character will finally be complete. It's with this hope in view that we seek to live in a way that's pure. This is the only motive that will make change last.

READY TO TURN RIGHT

Over the past few chapters, we've looked back to what Christ has done for us, and how his Spirit is at work in us. We've looked around us at our circumstances. We've looked down the left fork—our negative responses, and the desires that drive them. So how do we go about actually taking the right fork—choosing moment by moment to do the right thing? That's where the next three chapters are going.

THE MORE YOU KNOW?

So how does ongoing change happen? We tend to think that if we just know the right things, change will follow. It's the approach taken by the public service commercials on American TV. The commercial briefly describes the social problem (teenage pregnancy, obesity, heart disease) and then provides some helpful advice to address the problem. The commercial always ends with this statement: "The more you know." In other words, *Right thinking will lead to right behavior.* We might call this a cognitive/behavioral approach.

Many professing Christians approach the Christian life in the same way. The thinking is that if you struggle with worry, lust, gossip, greed, anger, or addictions (you pick your problem), the best way to change is through awareness and information. "The more you know..."

It's true that knowledge is important. If that weren't true, then writing and reading this book would be useless! Change won't come if we don't think rightly. But there is so much more to it than facts. After all, I know how I ought to treat my wife; but sometimes I don't treat her in the way I know I should. I know what the speed limit on the freeway is; that knowledge alone does not mean I will change my driving habits. There must be another dynamic in addition to right thinking.

IT'S ALL ABOUT RELATIONSHIP

At first sight it might seem that Paul agrees with the cognitive/behavioral approach. He says in Romans 12 v 2:

> *Do not conform to the pattern of this world, but be transformed by the renewing of your mind. Then you will be able to test and approve what God's will is—his good, pleasing and perfect will.*

So, renewing your mind leads to transformation, right? Not quite—because when Paul talks about the mind, he's talking not just about our intellectual capacity, but our inner person. If we were neuroscientists, we might say that Paul is speaking about the linkage between the rational brain and the emotional brain. But actually, Paul's talking about something spiritual here—any biological change is enabled by God's grace anyway! He is describing the part of someone that makes them tick: the central core of who a person is and what they live for. For Paul, if you are not changed at the core of who you are, change in your behavior will not follow. Real change begins at the level of what we honor, treasure, adore, and worship on a daily basis.

This is how commentator William Hendriksen states what Paul means in these verses:

> *Paul does not say, "Substitute one outward fashion for another." ... What is needed is "transformation," inner change, the renewing of the mind, that is, not only of the organ of thinking and reasoning but of the inner disposition; better still, of the heart, the inner being.*
>
> *(William Hendriksen, Romans, p 406)*

In other words, change must happen at a deeper level than just thinking and behaving.

What does this look like practically? It is more than talking to yourself and trying to convince yourself to change. It involves more than telling yourself to not worry, or get angry, or look at pornography because it is wrong. It is more than thinking positive thoughts (even biblical ones). It is even more than reminding yourself of who you are in Christ! It involves *talking to and relating to Christ* in the midst of your anxiety, anger, and addiction, or whatever your battle is. Since God is personal, change will be the result of you relating to him personally as you struggle. When you relate to Jesus in this way, gratitude and joy for his grace begin to work their way down deep into your soul. This is what drives true change! Relating to Jesus in this way could be called Christian meditation. It can be done alone in a quiet place or right in the middle of a hectic day—essentially, this word describes what it means to enter into a relationship and converse with a personal, loving, gracious God.

So here is the right way to approach change: right relating to God based upon right thinking about God will lead to right living before God. This does not mean it will be easy to overcome your struggles, nor does it mean that change will happen automatically or quickly. Rather, it will happen gradually over time. But it will happen.

UNION WITH CHRIST: THE KEY TO EVERYTHING

Theologians have a phrase to capture this idea of a relationship with Christ; they call it "union with Christ." The apostle Paul calls it being "in Christ." He uses this term approximately 165 times in his letters. That means it must be pretty important.

Union with Christ involves two aspects: legal and personal. We are made right with God in terms of our standing before him. Our union with Christ means that his track record becomes our track record, and so we receive a "not guilty" verdict before God. This is legal. But that's not the only sense in which we are united to Christ. We are also united to him in an ongoing relationship because the Holy Spirit takes up residence in our souls and connects us to God. This is personal. The best human analogy is marriage. When you get married, there is a legal aspect and a personal aspect—both are true and both are important.

There are many passages that highlight different aspects of this new status and relationship that we have with God. One such place is Ephesians 1, which starts with these words:

> *Praise be to the God and Father of our Lord Jesus Christ, who has blessed us in the heavenly realms with every spiritual blessing in Christ.* *(v 3)*

Paul then goes on to list these "spiritual blessings"—these are all ways of describing the many facets of our new relationship with God. And the implications for daily living are profound.

So let's count our blessings. Below is a list of nine blessings that are true of you if you are "in Christ" for you to slow down and meditate on. Modern research shows that thoughtful meditation can increase gratitude, and that being in awe of something can produce the emotion of humility. Of course, both of those dynamics—awe and gratitude—are at play as you worship God. Modern research involving high-tech brain imaging is simply confirming what God has already told us is good for us!

When you begin to savor what kind of relationship you have with God, you are more willing, able, and ready to demolish anything that is keeping you from growing and becoming more like Jesus. So as you read the list, take a moment to talk to God and thank him for how he has made it possible for you to enjoy knowing him and relating to him in the micro-moments of daily life.

CHOSEN AND PREDESTINED (EPHESIANS 1 v 4, 11)

Before you ever came into existence, God chose you to be his very dear child. The idea of being predestined or chosen does not imply that there was something special about you. No, just the opposite. Like Israel in the Old Testament, you were not the most impressive but the least. You were not on the top of the pile but at the bottom of the heap! This means you can feel built up without being puffed up. He chose you because he loves you. *In view of the nature of your relationship with God, talk to him now and thank him for his grace. You are not alone in the universe.*

CALLED (EPHESIANS 4 v 1, 4)

By his Spirit, God began to draw you to himself long before you ever started thinking about moving in his direction. Although you were hostile to him, God did not leave you to your own destructive devices; he called you (2 v 3-5). He called you because he loves you. *In view of the nature of your relationship with God, talk to him now and thank him for his grace. You were sought after by God.*

MADE ALIVE/REGENERATED (EPHESIANS 2 v 4-5)

As part of the process of being called, you were given new, spiritual life, which enabled you to confess your sins and place your trust and hope in Jesus. This is what the Bible calls being "born again." The Spirit of God made you alive when you were spiritually dead in your sin and utterly helpless. He gave you the desire to know him because he loves you. *In view of the nature of your relationship with God, talk to him now and thank him for his grace. You are no longer powerless and enslaved to sin.*

JUSTIFIED (EPHESIANS 1 v 7; ROMANS 5 v 1)

As a result of your initial trust in Christ, your sins were forgiven because Jesus died to pay the penalty for those sins. But there is even more. You are now viewed by God as if you have lived a perfect life, because Jesus lived a perfect life in your place. Not only has your debt been erased, but you have been given all of Christ's assets—his righteousness. So you can step off the treadmill of perfectionism and enjoy freedom. God forgave your sins and treats you as righteous because he loves you. *In view of the nature of your relationship with God, talk to him now and thank him for his grace. You are fully accepted by God and you don't have to earn his favor.*

ADOPTED (EPHESIANS 1 v 5)

At the very moment that you trusted in Christ, you were "adopted" by God. You have moved out of the courthouse, where he sits as Judge, and you have been welcomed into the family home, where he embraces you as your Father. Consider how intimate that is. You have also become part of a large family of brothers and sisters who are all united to Jesus: the body of Christ. And the Holy Spirit is within you, enabling you to talk to God as your

Father day by day. God adopted you because he loves you. *In view of the nature of your relationship with God, talk to him now and thank him for his grace. You are no longer isolated; you have the Father and the family you always wanted.*

ONGOING CHANGE (EPHESIANS 1 v 4, 13-14)
Now that God has adopted you, he is committed to sanctifying you—making you more like Jesus. He has given you the Holy Spirit, who gives you a new power and ability to fight sin through the practice of daily repentance and faith. Many times the path is slow and difficult; at other times you experience "growth spurts." And although every single day you fail and need to come to God for forgiveness, every single day he will grant it. He will not give up on you. He is changing you because he loves you. *In view of the nature of your relationship with God, talk to him now and thank him for his grace. You are no longer preprogrammed to sin. You do not need to stay stuck. You can change!*

HOPE IN SUFFERING (EPHESIANS 3 v 13)
God loves you so much, and is so committed to making you like Christ, that he's prepared to use any means to do it. And sometimes, that involves suffering (1 Peter 1 v 6-9). Jesus said that since he suffered, his followers will suffer too. But when difficult times come, you are not alone. You are not being punished. God is refining you like gold in a fire. Christ is with you in your suffering, and he is able to empathize and bring comfort because he loves you. *In view of the nature of your relationship with God, talk to him now and thank him for his grace. You will not be overcome by your suffering.*

PERSEVERANCE (EPHESIANS 1 v 13-14; 2 v 10)
God is going to finish what he started in you (Philippians 1 v 6). You are in a spiritual war that will not end until you

die or Jesus returns (Ephesians 6 v 10-18). Your enemies are the world (the world around us that is at odds with God), the flesh (remaining sin in you that is not yet completely eradicated), and the devil (the one who would love to derail your faith). But those who truly belong to Jesus will never be defeated. No one can snatch you from the Father's hand once you belong to him (John 10 v 28). So take courage as you continue to fight the good fight. He will never let go of you because he loves you. *In view of the nature of your relationship with God, talk to him now and thank him for his grace. God is working in you to enable you to persevere until the very end.*

GLORIFICATION (EPHESIANS 1 v 10, 13-14)

And as if all of this were not enough, you have his promise that one day you will be completely transformed into the glorious likeness of Jesus. You will spend eternity in the company of the true and living God (Father, Son, and Holy Spirit) as well as with your brothers and sisters in Christ, in a wonderful new creation. One day, all the traces of sin will be done away with and joy will be all that remains! God will wipe away every tear and completely eradicate sin and suffering because he loves you. *In view of the nature of your relationship with God, talk to him now and thank him for his grace. The restoration of all things, including yourself, is coming.*

These nine glorious realities are true of you if you are united to Christ by faith—it is these truths which define your relationship with him. As you dwell on these realities, they should do two things. First, they should cause you to rest and be thankful that God has provided all you need to experience his love. Second, they should make you restless and eager to grow in grace so that you can reflect God's glory more and more brightly.

WORK IT THROUGH

It's easier to reflect on these things right now when things are calm, and you are looking at them on the page in front of you. It is much harder to do so in the moment when life is moving so fast. That is why we need to constantly be reminded of these truths.

Take a moment and read back over the nine blessings that are yours because of your relationship with Jesus. What is it that you are struggling with right now? What temptation or hardship is on your mind at the moment? As you read back through the list and give thanks, allow the weight of his love for you to bring comfort, encouragement, new resolve, and growing hope as you face your specific temptations and trials.

I would encourage you to read the whole of Ephesians to get a sense of the broader context of these blessings. Choose some key verses and write them down on a card to keep on your person, or put them in your phone and set a reminder, so that you can reflect on your relationship with Jesus throughout your day. In the next two chapters, we'll think more about how our relationship with Jesus can reshape and change us in the every day.

Remember, change is all about relationship. Right relating to God based upon right thinking about God will lead to right living before God. Skills and techniques can be useful, but nothing is more vital than your connection to Christ.

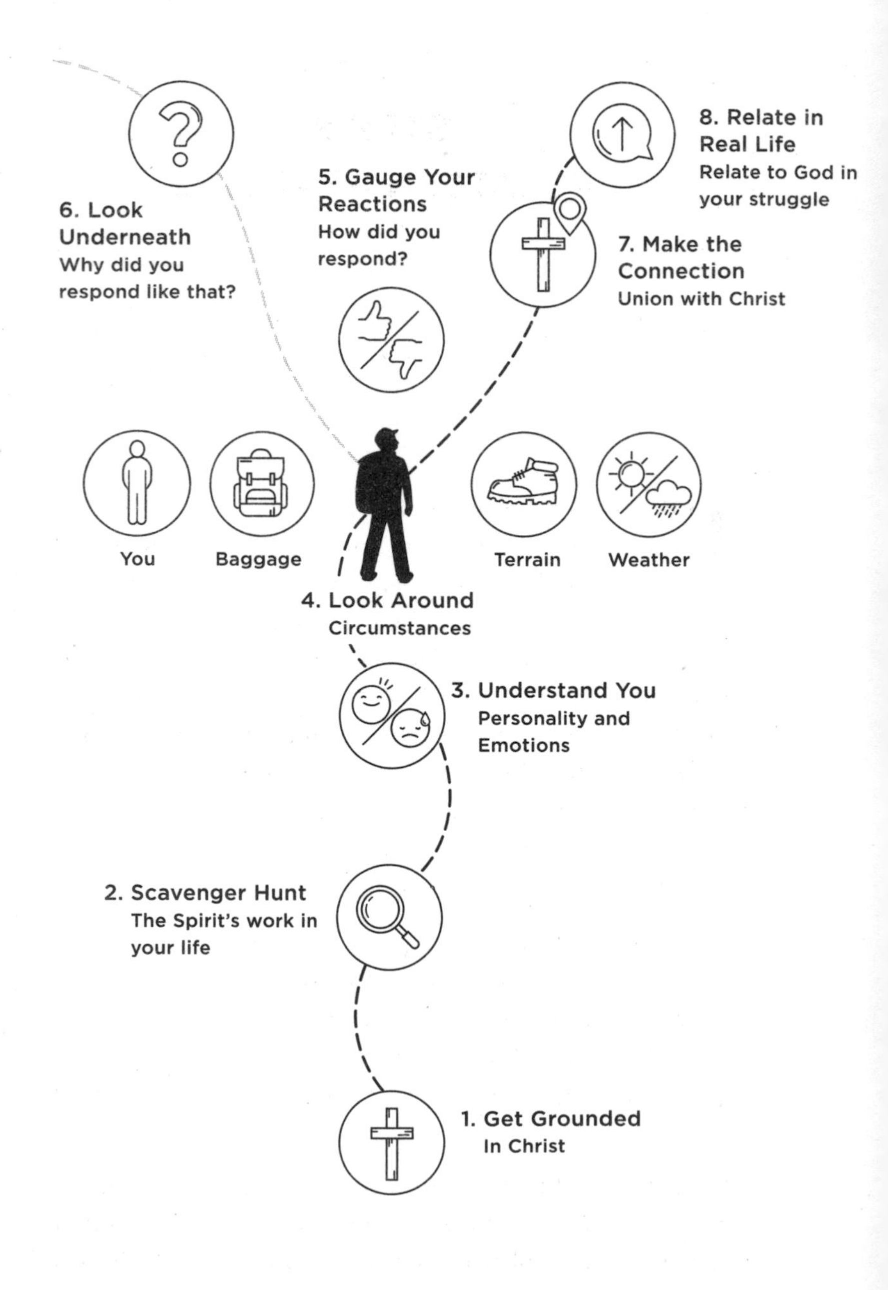
6. Look Underneath
Why did you respond like that?
5. Gauge Your Reactions
How did you respond?
8. Relate in Real Life
Relate to God in your struggle
7. Make the Connection
Union with Christ
You
Baggage
Terrain
Weather
4. Look Around
Circumstances
3. Understand You
Personality and Emotions
2. Scavenger Hunt
The Spirit's work in your life
1. Get Grounded
In Christ

STEP 8
RELATE IN REAL LIFE

Relate to God in your struggle based on your union with Christ.

In the previous chapter, we saw that change is all about relationship—specifically, your relationship with God, which is grounded in your union with Christ. The process of change is not primarily a discipline or technique. Nor is it even a case of thinking positive thoughts about your new standing in Christ. Though those things may be a part of the process, it is a conscious relating to Christ based on what he has done for you that is fundamental. He is a person. You can talk to him. This is where real strength for the journey is found. The writer of Hebrews describes what that looks like in Hebrews 4 v 15-16:

> *For we do not have a high priest who is unable to empathize with our weaknesses, but we have one who has been tempted in every way, just as we are—yet he did not sin. Let us then approach God's throne of grace with confidence, so that we may receive mercy and find grace to help us in our time of need.*

Jesus has identified with your weakness and wants to help you—he knows what you are going through. You can relate to God with confidence in your time of need or temptation! How? Only by the fact that you are united to Christ! His standing before the Father is your standing before the Father. Jesus' track record is perfect—"he did not sin"—and that's how God sees you, too.

Step 7 on our journey of change was to focus on the various ways that we are connected to Jesus. Now we need to bring these truths into the real-life fight to grow in grace. So here is the challenge: how do we take the truth of our union with Christ and utilize it in such a way that we relate to God during our struggle, and therefore actually change? That's Step 8.

GOSPEL DECONSTRUCTION: REPENTANCE

Your union with Christ should move you in two ways: a lifestyle of repentance (or "deconstruction") and of faith (or "reconstruction"). What does this look like?

I'll start by sharing an example from my own life—follow along as I highlight a few themes from the previous chapters. (You will get to do this for yourself later.)

LOOK AROUND YOU (STEP 4)

Late one afternoon, I was sitting in my house enjoying some peace and quiet. This always works better when no one else is around to interrupt you! At just the moment that I was contemplating how peaceful it was, the front door opened and then was quickly slammed. I immediately felt tense and a bit agitated. It was my teenage daughter coming home from school. I managed to welcome her home by saying, "Hey, how was your day?" I got a terse response: "Why would you care?" She proceeded to stomp up one flight of stairs, then stomp down the hallway and stomp up the second flight of stairs. Then I heard it again: she slammed her bedroom door! What was a peaceful, quiet afternoon in the house was shattered in about 15 seconds.

GAUGE YOUR REACTIONS (STEP 5)

I could feel myself tense up immediately. There was that all too familiar struggle with irritation and anger. It was a personal battle within that occasionally spilled over into my interpersonal relationships. It was as if I was standing at the junction: would I respond in the right way?

LOOK UNDERNEATH (STEP 6)

Why was I irritated? What was I not getting that I wanted? On the surface, there was nothing inherently sinful in my desires. But in that moment, they had become something that I was living for, or worshiping, more than Christ:

- *Peace and comfort:* I had been working with people all day and all I wanted was some downtime from the challenges of what other people wanted. Drinking a diet coke and catching up on the daily news on TV was bliss. As soon as my daughter had entered the house, the atmosphere was ruined. Peace and comfort, which can be very good things, had morphed into something I was living for.
- *Appreciation and respect:* Who doesn't want appreciation, especially from your own son or daughter? After all the sacrifices you make for them, the least they could do is show respect! In this instance I felt disrespected when my daughter did not respond positively to my greeting. Appreciation and respect, which can be very good things, had morphed into something I was living for.

WHY GOOD THINGS MAKE BAD GODS

So the stage was set for the demolition process. This is where Scripture begins to lay you bare and bring you face to face with the problem within your own heart. We've already looked at two passages that illuminate the deadly nature of taking something good in creation and making it what you worship or live for in the moment.

> *They exchanged the truth of God for a lie, and worshiped and served created things rather than the Creator—who is forever praised.* (Romans 1 v 25)

Paul is describing the disposition of someone who does not believe in God, but this same dynamic is true of every Christian as we fight against remaining sin. Even though all the blessings that we receive through our union with Christ are true and real, the battle continues. That is why John says this to Christians in 1 John 5 v 21: "Dear children, keep yourselves from idols." He reminds us that Christians also face the temptation to make something in creation what we live for, adore, and revolve our lives around.

> *Do not store up for yourselves treasures on earth, where moths and vermin destroy, and where thieves break in and steal ... For where your treasure is, there your heart will be also.* (Matthew 6 v 19-21)

Jesus says that when you make something in this world what you treasure, your loyalty will be first and foremost to it and not to him. When you do this, all your energies will go into protecting and focusing on that treasure. This will ripple out into how you live your life and how you treat others.

Scripture shows me what my problem was: in that moment, I was treasuring good things like peace, comfort, and respect more than I was treasuring Christ. As a result, it expressed itself in my personal attitudes and my behavior toward my daughter.

WHAT'S UNDER THE HOOD DRIVES THE GAUGE OF BEHAVIOR

I proceeded to get up out of my chair and stomp up the first flight of stairs. As I was doing this, I asked myself, "Where did my daughter learn to stomp upstairs like she just did?" At the time I didn't even realize the obvious answer!

Why was I doing what I was doing? Because the peace, comfort, appreciation, and respect that I was adoring had been so quickly taken from me. My peace was upended, my comfort was challenged, and my need for appreciation and respect had been unheeded. My little universe, where I ruled as my own king and got what I wanted, had come crashing down. All it took was my own daughter walking in the front door to bring my idols toppling down!

And when they were taken from me, I began to react in sinful ways. Here are just a few sinfully angry responses that were bubbling under the surface.

- *Angry comment #1:* "Children should obey their parents in the Lord! That's what Ephesians 6 v 1 says. Don't you come into this house, slam doors, and stomp upstairs!"
- *Angry comment #2:* "Have you forgotten the fifth commandment, which says you are to honor your parents? If you don't respond to me when I speak to you, there will be serious consequences!"
- *Angry comment #3:* "How dare you slam doors and stomp upstairs in this house? I work hard to provide a roof over your head. You need to think about that the next time you come in this house and speak to me like that!"
- *Angry comment #4:* "Don't you ever enter this house again and dismiss my kind greetings. That is completely inappropriate and will not be tolerated going forward! Do you hear me?!"

Have you ever found yourself thinking and saying things like this? You can tell that I have! These are words and actions that slowly kill relationships. They thrive on guilt and shame to win the day. But this is what we sound like when we are worshiping a false god. Only the grace and kindness of God can melt a proud parent's heart like mine and utterly change their speech. Thankfully, that is what happened on this occasion.

GOSPEL RECONSTRUCTION: FAITH

As I stomped up those stairs, I said in my mind, "Help me, God. Here I go again." The words were simple, but they were based on rich truths that were planted in my heart. It was as if I was saying, *Oh God, help me in my time of need. Temptation is upon me and I am not up to the challenge. I need your grace and power to live and act differently. I know I am united to Jesus. So please, prevent me from straying from you. You have promised to give me mercy and grace in my time of need. And that time is now!*

This is where the reconstruction began. It started with a desperate cry for help to God and continued into ongoing conversation with him. It just happened that I had been doing some sermon preparation earlier that morning on a passage in 1 Corinthians 1. (Of course, these things never "just happen"!) The one verse that stood out was 1 Corinthians 1 v 30:

> *It is because of [God] that you are in Christ Jesus, who has become for us wisdom from God—that is, our righteousness, holiness and redemption.*

That verse captures a host of the blessings that we discussed in the previous chapter. And as I studied it, it had begun to penetrate deep into my soul. It was beautiful in its simplicity. It captured so many of the blessings that were mine because I was in Christ. These truths enabled me to start talking to God, and turn from gazing at daily pleasures like peace, comfort, appreciation, and respect, and start gazing at Christ.

So as I rounded the corner at the top of the first flight of stairs and uttered my simple prayer—"Help me, God. Here I go again"—something astonishing happened. What followed was utterly miraculous, though no one would have been able to see the transformation that was going on in my soul at that moment. Here is how it unfolded:

- By God's grace, I was beginning to see how I was living for peace, comfort, and respect rather than for Christ. Seeing patterns and signature temptations is a work of the Spirit.
- I started to cry out to God for help. This simple pivot took me out of myself and directly to God.
- I began to talk to God based on 1 Corinthians 1 v 30. The truth of Scripture began at the "head level" but moved to a deeper place. I began to relate to God. The written word enabled me to engage with God and talk to him.
- The truths in that one verse reminded me of my connection to Christ. They captured who I was in Christ and how that was deeper, more profound, and more beautiful than anything else in this world—even good things like peace, comfort, appreciation, and respect!

The ensuing conversation I had with God happened within seconds, yet it changed everything. Here is an "extended version" to show you what it sounded like. Notice how I am comparing my idols with the grace of God for me in Christ as expressed in 1 Corinthians 1 v 30:

> *Father, you say that in Christ I am* ***righteous****. I am forgiven, justified, and adopted. That is amazing! I am completely*

accepted by you because of what Jesus has done for me. You will never snub me or turn away from me. Why, then, am I so upset that my daughter has displayed disrespect to me? Lord, thank you and help me!

Father, you say that in Christ I am ***holy****. I am called, born again, given new life, and given the Spirit of adoption. I have a new heart and a new power at work in me by the Holy Spirit. I don't have to keep sinning in the same old way, because you are at work in me. I don't have to let my desires for comfort and appreciation drive my life. Lord, thank you and help me!*

Father, you say that in Christ I have ***redemption****. I have been bought with the price of the precious blood of Jesus, and you will persevere to the end. One day, Jesus is going to come again, and I will play a part in ruling over your new creation, where there will be no more sin, suffering, or sorrow. Why am I so upset that I have lost some sense of control over this little plot of real estate that I don't even own; the bank does?! Lord, thank you and help me!*

EXPERIENCING DEEP CHANGE

As I was relating to God like this, something began to happen. The allure of earthly peace, comfort, and respect began to lose its attractiveness and charm. Instead, Jesus in all his grace and power began to loom larger on the horizon of my heart. I found myself worshiping and thanking God for his kindness to me. The irritation and anger began to dissipate. It was being replaced with joy, gratitude, patience, empathy, and love. I was experiencing deep renewal as I engaged in repentance (turning away from peace, comfort, and respect) and faith (turning to Christ and his loving kindness).

As I turned the corner, I found myself walking calmly up the second flight of stairs. The grace of Jesus was changing my behavior even to the level of how I used my legs and feet to walk a set of stairs! Another miraculous thing happened as I approached my daughter's door. Rather than using my fist to hit the door in anger, I was able to pivot my hand and simply tap on the door with my knuckles. The process of internal change is a mystery at one level, and yet something in which we clearly participate.

This simple illustration from my own life represents the micro-moments of change. Of course, this example is a relatively low-level issue. But most often, the war against our "big" struggle is won through a series of "little" battles. It is in these seemingly simple moments of life where change becomes real. And if we can't relate to God in the more mundane moments of life, we will not relate to him when the more significant moments arise.

MOCKING YOUR FALSE OBJECT OF WORSHIP

Another helpful way to dismantle your false objects of worship "in the moment" is to mock them. The Old Testament prophets show us what that looks like. The prophets were prosecutors, showing Israel how they had violated God's loving commands by worshiping false gods. To get Israel's attention, the prophets would sometimes use mockery to show how useless these idols were. One example of this is in Jeremiah 10 v 1-16. Verses 5 and 6 are particularly compelling:

"Like a scarecrow in a cucumber field,
their idols cannot speak;
they must be carried
because they cannot walk.
Do not fear them;

they can do no harm
nor can they do any good."
No one is like you, L*ORD;*
you are great,
and your name is mighty in power.

Through mockery, Jeremiah is demolishing the supposed power of Israel's idols—they're useless compared to the living God! That is what we can do too—we must compare our false objects of worship with the true Person we should be worshiping. Using the example between me and my daughter, here is how that could play out:

- "Diet coke and TV news," when did you ever humble yourself and take on human flesh to identify with my temptations and struggles?
- "Peace and quiet," when did you ever suffer in my place, so that you might identify with my sufferings?
- "Respect," when were you ever raised from the dead to win my reconciliation with God?
- "Appreciation," when did you ever promise to return and wipe away every tear and restore all things?

Mocking our idols shifts our gaze from something that we thought looked beautiful (comfort, peace, appreciation, respect) and places before us someone more beautiful: the incarnate, suffering, dying, risen, conquering Savior! This is the dynamic that changes lives in deep and profound ways.

WORK IT THROUGH

Think about a recent incident when you responded to circumstances in an unhelpful or sinful way.

- What would it have looked like instead if you had related to God in that moment? Write out your own "extended version" of how that could have sounded, like the one on pages 113-114.

- What were the idols that you were valuing more highly than Christ in that moment? What would it look like to "mock" those false objects of worship? Write out your own taunts, like the ones on page 116.

So what happened between me and my daughter when I got to the top of the stairs? We'll come back to that on Step 9...

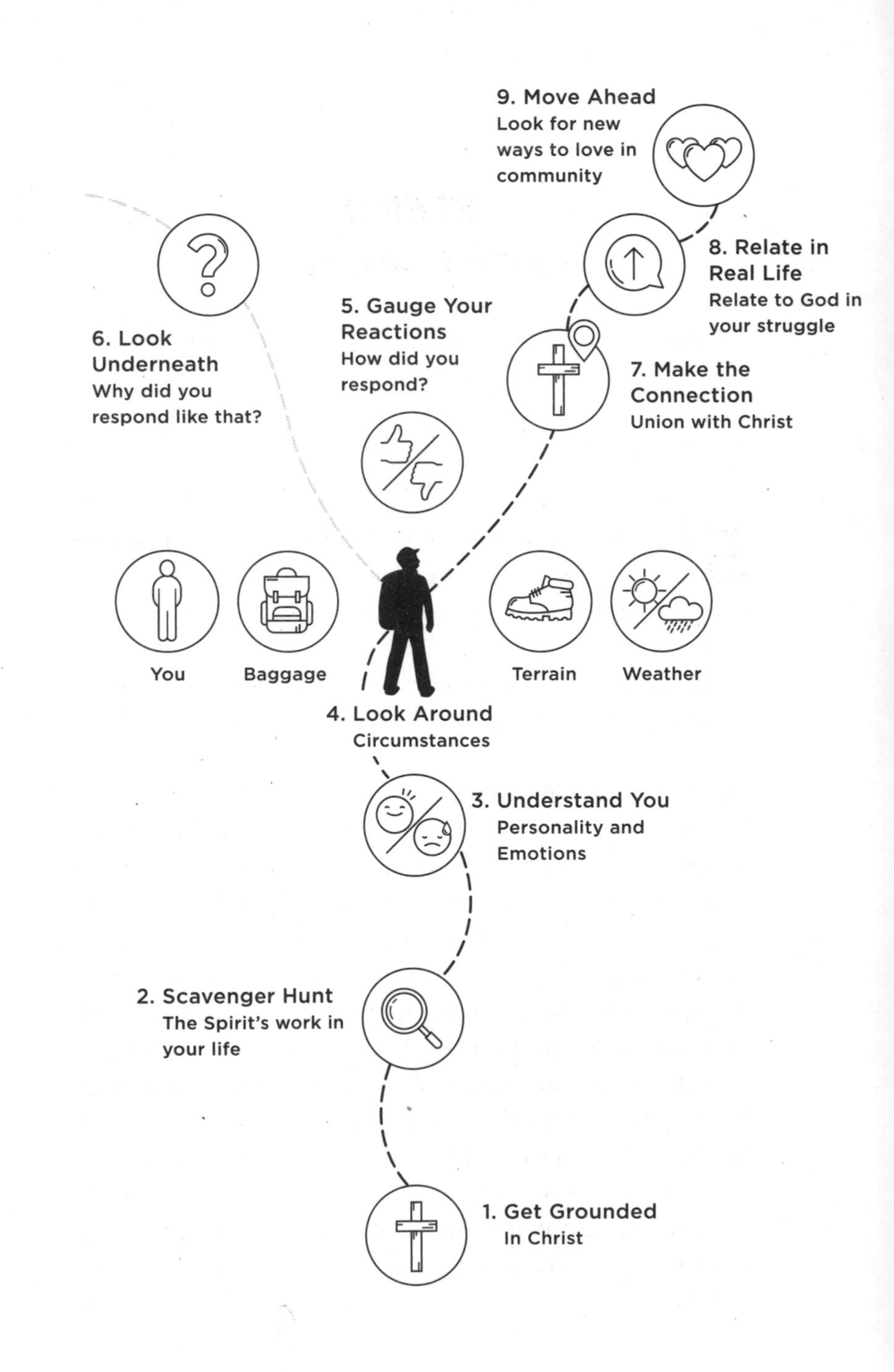
9. Move Ahead
Look for new ways to love in community
8. Relate in Real Life
Relate to God in your struggle
7. Make the Connection
Union with Christ
6. Look Underneath
Why did you respond like that?
5. Gauge Your Reactions
How did you respond?
You
Baggage
Terrain
Weather
4. Look Around
Circumstances
3. Understand You
Personality and Emotions
2. Scavenger Hunt
The Spirit's work in your life
1. Get Grounded
In Christ

STEP 9
MOVE AHEAD

Look for new opportunities to love others for the long term.

So far we've covered eight steps that help us to choose the "right fork" at our junction. And I hope that by now you've been encouraged by some victories in your battle, however small.

But… then what? In those moments when we do respond to circumstances in the right way, what happens next?

PLAY THE LONG GAME

Let me continue to tell you what transpired once I got to my daughter's bedroom. Immediately after tapping on the door (instead of banging in anger), I was able to say in a calm voice, "How are you doing and would you like to talk?" An amazing change had transpired in me. My body language, tone of voice, emotions, choice of words, and how I knocked on the door had been radically altered. The drama of redemption had played out in my life and my daughter had no idea that she had been rescued from me because I had been rescued from myself… by God's gracious help.

Yet as soon as those calm words came out of my mouth, my daughter responded in a way that might surprise and frustrate you: "Go away! I don't want to talk to anyone, not even you!"

Wow! Now I was faced with a new situation. How would I respond to her response? Would I become self-righteous on the heels of my transformation? "How can she act that way toward me, especially after I was so godly?" It almost sounds funny, doesn't it? Thankfully, I was able to respond in a quiet manner with these words: "That's fine; if you want to talk, I'll be downstairs. Dinner will be ready in an hour."

Sometimes we will choose the path of obedience and find that we still don't get what we hope for. Our attempts at change will sometimes go unappreciated. Maybe your spouse doesn't even notice the efforts you make at de-escalating a conflict. Or perhaps you've offered an apology to someone for your behavior in the past, but they've continued to spurn it.

And this isn't just the case in our relationships with other people—sometimes we'll end up frustrated at ourselves, too. We'll find that our sin clings tight, and that our small victories are just one battle in a larger war. Maybe you've managed to go a whole week without pornography—but you find that the unwanted images continue to replay in your mind. Or if you struggle with anxiety, you might be encouraged by your response to one stressful situation, only to be thrown off course by the next. When that happens, we need to keep in mind the big picture. We need to play the long game.

In one given moment, there's usually only a small difference between the left and right paths. But if we keep choosing right, time after time, our lives will end up in a different place altogether than if we'd kept choosing the left path. It's about long-term difference. Sometimes, we'll still do the wrong thing—we'll "go left." But it's the bigger picture that matters. And the more we go right, the easier it is to go right next time. The left path starts to look more "overgrown" as our habits change.

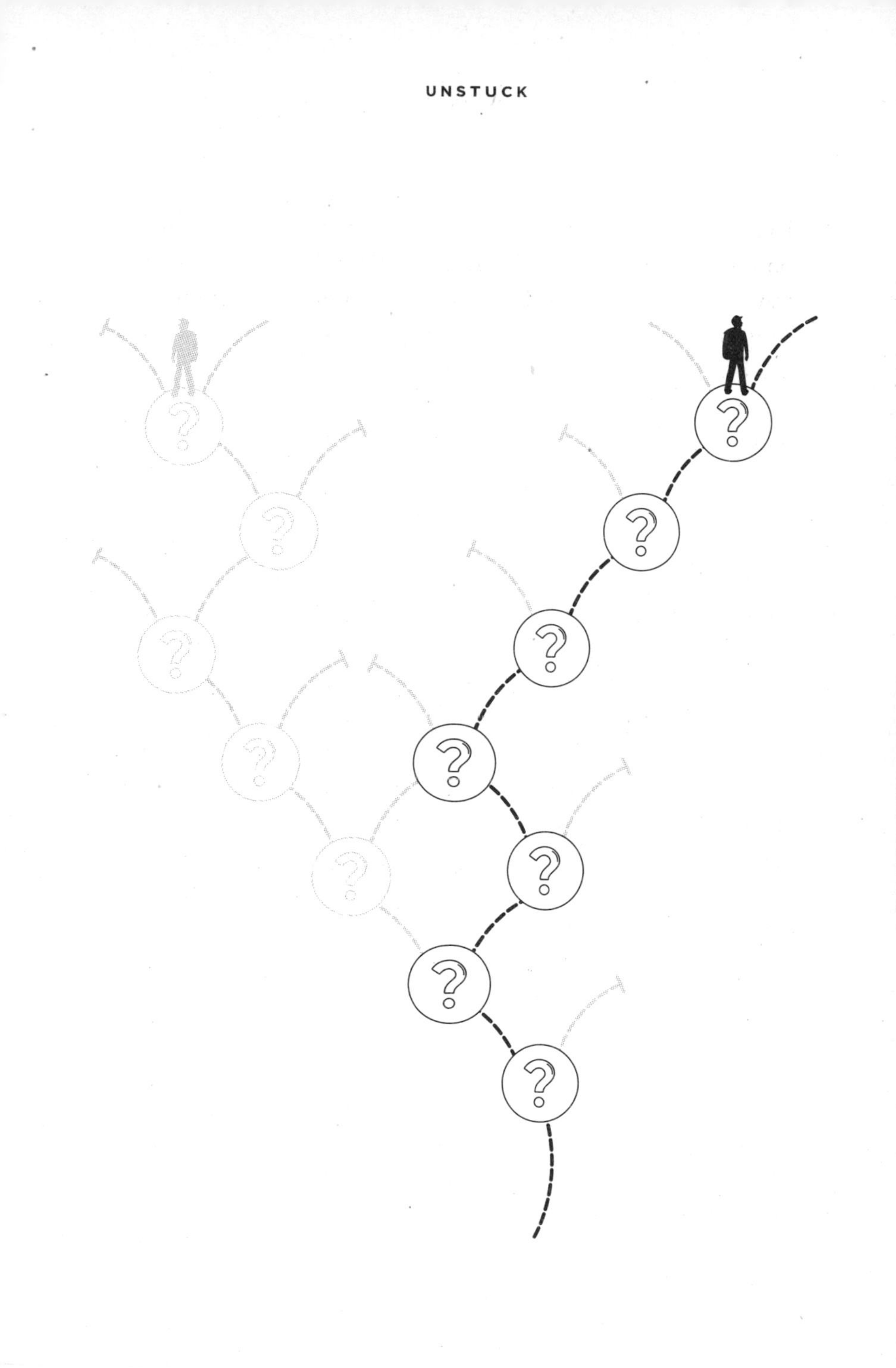

Imagine if my daughter grew up in a family where, for 18 years, her father was always dropping the hammer. Imagine, though, if she grew up in a family where, for 18 years, her father was growing in grace and showing humility and patience, albeit imperfectly. These little moments may seem inconsequential, but not when you view them within the larger perspective of months and years. These two father/daughter relationships may not look that different early on, but they will look radically different over the course of many years. That is the larger perspective we need to have when we consider the process of growth in grace. Every little moment counts!

LOOK FOR NEW OPPORTUNITIES TO LOVE

After my patience with my daughter went unnoticed and I received an angry response from the other side of her bedroom door, I was able to still go down the path to the right: I proceeded to calmly and quietly walk down the stairs and help my wife with dinner. At this point, it felt as if everything was over, but it wasn't. About an hour later, my daughter came down the stairs and joined us for dinner. She seemed to be in a better place. After dinner, as we were cleaning up, I was able to ask her about her day at school.

As she shared with me, I began to understand why she had entered the house earlier that day in such an agitated mood. She began to tell me about a few friends who had said some harsh things about her that hurt her feelings. She had had a "mean girl" day at school. In addition, I was aware that she was very self-conscious about her skin. She was experiencing normal changes, but the result was frustration and insecurity about her appearance. These were no small issues to easily dismiss.

As soon as she began to share about her day, it dawned on me that her entering the house and stomping up the stairs had *nothing* to do with me! And yet in the moment I had been making it *all* about me. Making good things a god can turn you into a self-centered tyrant!

And with the Spirit's help, I was able to see what was really going on. This vulnerable thirteen-year-old girl was trying to navigate her way through the ups and downs of being a human being in a broken world. She was experiencing the warfare of life on this planet. By God's grace, I had not taken my anger out on her, and that meant that I now had the opportunity to love her instead. I listened to her, asked her thoughtful questions, and spoke reassuringly.

Change isn't just about stopping doing something, but about actively loving people. For example, the aim of overcoming our anxiety isn't just so that we feel better, but so that we can be more wholeheartedly focused on serving other people. Our view of the Christian life mustn't be reduced to following negative commands that scream at us, "Do not do that!" It is much bigger and more positive. The call is to personally grow so that we more fully reflect God's kindness and love to others, as an overflow of the love we have experienced from him. Ephesians 4 v 22-24 instructs us to "put off your old self, which is being corrupted by its deceitful desires; to be made new in the attitude of your minds; and to put on the new self, created to be like God in true righteousness and holiness." In every situation, there is a positive response to pursue as well as a negative response to avoid.

As you can see, change has both a personal and practical dynamic. It is personal because, for a Christian, it grows out of a very personal relationship with God. It also happens within an interpersonal context with other people. Change is practical too. Since sin and disobedience are very specific and concrete attitudes and actions, growth in grace must be as specific and concrete. In other words, grace-based change will always be very visible because it shapes the way you live life in your body within the context of your relationships. Change changes things in real life!

So as you begin to respond to your circumstances differently, you will find that you have new opportunities to do good to others in very real and tangible ways, as I was able to do with my daughter. Look for these opportunities and seize them.

EMBRACE CHANGE IN COMMUNITY

The process of change is deeply personal, but it is not individualistic. In fact, change happens within two relational contexts. The first is our relationship with God. That is what we have focused on in this book: how do I grow in grace as I relate to God throughout the seemingly mundane moments of everyday life?

But there is a second relational context: our relationships with others. We cannot ignore that community is a powerful and prominent theme in Scripture. No personal problem is ever only private. My personal struggles and battles always impact my relationships. And God has designed us so that those relationships are the context in which we can be helped, encouraged, challenged, and prayed for. True and lasting change requires us to be in meaningful relationships with other believers in order for that growth to take place.

Hebrews 3 v 12-13 shows us that we need the constant encouragement of our brothers and sisters in order to stay on the right path and avoid sin.

> *See to it, brothers and sisters, that none of you has a sinful, unbelieving heart that turns away from the living God. But encourage one another daily, as long as it is called "Today," so that none of you may be hardened by sin's deceitfulness.*

Due to my ongoing battle with indwelling sin, I need others to help me see when I am being blinded or deceived by it. Christian fellowship is a gift that has a side to it that, on the surface, does not seem all that enjoyable! But when done well and in love, the challenge of another believer can be life-giving. Proverbs 27 v 6 says, "Wounds from a friend can be trusted, but an enemy multiplies kisses." You need others to tell you the truth in love about where you need to grow. Sometimes you cannot see this on your own, but often others can.

You also need your brothers and sisters to encourage you to keep fighting—to remind you that the battle against sin is a battle worth winning. You need them to keep warning you that the consequences of sin are deadly. And you need them to keep fixing your eyes on the "living God," your heavenly Father, who is full of grace and mercy toward those who repent.

In Hebrews 10 v 24-25 we see the other side of the coin too:

> *And let us consider how we may spur one another on toward love and good deeds, not giving up meeting together, as some are in the habit of doing, but encouraging one another—and all the more as you see the Day approaching.*

We don't just need others to turn us from sin; we're dependent on their ongoing encouragement to keep us moving in the other direction too, as we seek to actively grow in loving and serving others. Remember, the change process must be grounded in the two relational contexts: relationship with God, and relationship with brothers and sisters in Christ. If we want to change, we must be connected in a meaningful way to a local church. One important way that we receive the kind of encouragement that Hebrews is talking about is as we hear the word preached and we sing truth to one another Sunday by Sunday. But we also want to be fostering the kind of relationships with others where we "encourage one another daily" on a person-to-person level (3 v 13).

A TELLING QUESTION

Take a moment and ask yourself a very practical question. Do you have two or three people in your life right now who know you well? People who know your joys, sorrows, weaknesses, sinful inclinations, and the suffering you have experienced throughout your life? Do you have people who put that knowledge to good use by praying for you, inquiring about how you are doing, and asking how they might best help you? This is the surest test of whether you are truly living in community with other Christians.

If you are like me, you may find this very challenging. Perhaps you're so busy that you think you don't have time. Even if you go to worship services regularly and are involved in some kind of smaller group, it can still be hard to have conversations that move beyond small talk. So what can you do? Here are a few suggestions to try over the next few weeks:

- In one of your closest relationships, share something that is hard in your life, and ask that friend if they would pray regularly for you.
- Find someone who is interested in reading a book together that addresses an issue in your life that you are seeking to change.
- If you share prayer requests in your small group, seek to be intentionally vulnerable by sharing something more personal: maybe a struggle with gossip, anger, anxiety, or pride.
- The next time someone asks you how you are doing, avoid the polite response of "Fine" and share a bit

more with them. "I am feeling a little pressure at work with a situation, and I need someone to give me some advice and pray with me."

In all these examples, you want to try to take some of your relationships deeper. You have to be wise and patient as you do this. You don't want to come on too strong or you may make the other person run a mile! Again, the aim is to find one or two people who know you best at whatever level, and move the friendship to a more substantive place.

WORK IT THROUGH

Think of a specific area of struggle where you are seeking to change.

- Where do you hope to be in this area in one year's time, five years' time, and ten years' time? What might life look like if you continue growing? Allow this exercise to encourage you about what is possible long term, and to move you to pray for your future.
- Think about a time when you have resisted sin in the past week or so. What opportunities did this open up for you to love others? In what concrete ways would you like to increasingly love others as you continue to grow and change? Again, talk to God and ask for his help.
- Which Christian friends are you going to seek to deepen your relationship with? How are you going to start?

CASE STUDY
JIM AND ANXIETY

Jim's journey to change that lasts.

Now that we've come to the end of our nine-step journey, I want to provide a summary of where we have been, and encourage you with what is possible, by way of a case study. It is in no way exhaustive, but it should help you to start putting all the pieces together.

You might remember Jim from chapter 1. He is in his late forties, and when he first started meeting with me, he told me that he had struggled with anxiety for as long as he could remember. His anxiety would display itself in bursts of anger, obsessive controlling behaviors, and intense physiological symptoms (sweating, heart racing, agitation, etc.). Because this has been a long-term struggle, he wonders whether it is really possible that he will ever be different. He is stuck.

So what might it look like for Jim to walk our nine steps and move toward lasting change?

STEP 1: GET GROUNDED

Jim is discouraged and despondent, and wonders whether his faith in Christ is real. He sometimes questions if God truly loves him—it feels as if God is punishing him by keeping him in a constant struggle with worry. Jim is truly a Christian and depends upon Christ alone for his acceptance before God, but many times he has doubts.

Jim needs to be encouraged that abiding struggles with temptations and suffering are normal, and that Jesus has a firm grip on him and his life. Christ's love is consistent and persistent. He needs to gaze outward and upward to get his bearings and not focus solely on the battle with anxiety. He needs the words of an encouraging friend, and to regularly be reminded that "there is now no condemnation for those who are in Christ Jesus" (Romans 8 v 1). To put it simply, Jim needs to hear and remember the truth of the gospel every single day that he gets out of bed.

STEP 2: SCAVENGER HUNT

Jim has a hard time seeing how the Spirit is at work in his life. All he is tempted to see is how much he struggles with anxiety! It doesn't feel as if much is changing.

Jim will need the eyes of another to help him see what he does not. A brother or sister in Christ could point out how God's Spirit is actively enabling Jim to face each day, love his wife and children, stay connected to his local church, find moments of comfort in prayer and the Scriptures, faithfully get to work and serve his employees... and the list could go on. Jim needs to be encouraged to see that there are many small but important evidences of the Spirit at work in his life too.

STEP 3: UNDERSTAND YOU

When Jim compares himself to others who appear more confident and less anxious than him, his tendency is to think that there is something deeply flawed about his personality and his experience of emotions.

Jim needs help to see that we're all hardwired by God with a unique DNA, and that shows up in different personality strengths and weaknesses. Jim's strengths are his awareness of his environment. He can spot danger before anyone else! He is a great protector. In addition, his range of emotions makes him more naturally empathetic toward the burdens of others. Jim tends to be more patient and understanding of others who don't feel safe or "normal." Jim needs encouragement to see his unique personality and the strengths as well as the weaknesses it holds. He also needs to see that others likewise have strengths and weaknesses in this area; they are different and not necessarily better.

It is important for Jim to learn to express his emotions in a good and constructive way, even his "negative" emotions. Emotions that are suppressed don't go away; they fester under the surface and create more problems. Developing a strong emotional life will be an important part of Jim's journey.

STEP 4: LOOK AROUND

BODY

Brain: Jim was diagnosed with a learning disability when he was very young. As a result, he worked very hard to keep up with, and even excel ahead of, his classmates. His high performance academically became a way for Jim to stand out.

Due to some of Jim's relational history, the warning and emotional centers of his brain (amygdala and limbic region) tend to be very active. He is highly vigilant and on the look out for danger, especially from other people. There is also a history of mental illness in Jim's family and he has been on several medications for his anxiety. It is important for him to continue having the medication monitored by a trusted psychiatrist. Jim has also been encouraged to practice deep breathing exercises when he feels stressed. This allows him to slow down so he can fight unhelpful thought-patterns.

Body: Jim is not very athletic, and he is small in stature. As a result, Jim experienced varying degrees of bullying until he went to college. This was another situational factor which increased his level of anxiety.

Gender: Jim is a white male. This has provided certain advantages, although it does not negate the bullying he experienced growing up. As a man, he tends to express his anxiety and fear through anger. He will blow up if he feels that someone is creeping over into his lane on the highway. He can be volatile with his family, and they report not knowing which "Jim" will come home from work.

BAGGAGE

Event and relational history: Jim grew up in a family where his father was sometimes abusive verbally and physically. At the same time, he could also be very nurturing. He grew up never knowing which "father" would show up. One event with his mother stands out. He once brought a grade of 98% home and showed it to his mom. She replied by saying that it needed to be 100%. This only fueled his perfectionist tendencies. Jim was the oldest of four siblings and seems to have caught the brunt of his father's angry outbursts. A deep fear of abandonment and disapproval is always lurking just below the surface.

Socio-economic history: Jim grew up in a middle-income family but there was rarely any extra money for special occasions. He continues to express a fear of being fired and failing to provide for his family, even though he has never been fired in his 25-year work history.

Religious training: Jim grew up in a small town where church was the center of social activity. His family attended church but it was very legalistic with an emphasis on keeping rules. Jim's view of God has been tainted by his own experience with his father—he tends to think that

Jesus had to step in and go to the cross in order to protect us from an abusive heavenly Father. He is always wondering which heavenly Father is going to show up: the wrathful one or the nurturing one. His confidence in God's love is low and he lives in a state of underlying fear, which manifests itself in perfectionist tendencies.

TERRAIN

Current circumstances: Jim has recently changed jobs and moved his family to a new city. His new job involves managing about twelve people. In his previous role, he had no direct reports. He feels overwhelmed and is constantly interrupted at work with petty office politics and a range of HR issues to address. Life at home with three teenage children is also very challenging right now. Finally, Jim is in his late 50s and he is fearful that he will not have enough money in his 401k pension plan to retire.

WEATHER

The micro-moments and challenges of daily life: In view of all the above, Jim is currently struggling with intense anger. He finds that he is usually agitated with his employees, his children, and his wife. He gets angry when people are running late or do not meet his expectations. Hence his deep anxiety is negatively affecting almost all his relationships.

STEP 5: GAUGE YOUR REACTIONS

Physical sensations and emotions: Jim's anxiety often expresses itself in anger. If he feels threatened in any way, he moves into fight-or-flight mode; most often fight mode. When he does this, he experiences another wave of emotions—guilt and shame. This makes Jim feel hopeless. Sometimes this will lead to a season of exhaustion and mild depression.

Thinking patterns: Jim can find himself giving into catastrophizing thoughts. The fear of potential failure at work is overwhelming.

Beliefs: The background noise of Jim's belief system is that other people can't be trusted. Their care and love is fickle. Likewise, God seems capricious and unpredictable. He can't be trusted.

Behaviors: Jim tends to be hyper-vigilant and argumentative. He has a short fuse and will easily blow up at co-workers, other drivers on the highway, his wife, and his children. His perfectionistic tendencies make him a very controlling boss.

If you were Jim's friend or counselor, then all of this information about him should build your understanding of and empathy for him. Without it, your "help" may instead cause more guilt and damage. Taking the time to get to know a person's story is not a luxury; it is a necessity.

STEP 6: LOOK UNDERNEATH

As Jim begins to ask the "why?" and "what?" questions, his deeper loyalties emerge. The fundamental driver underneath most of Jim's behaviors is fear. He is afraid of God. Is God loving or full of wrath? He is afraid of other people. Are they safe or are they going to bully him? He is afraid of failure and of the future.

If God and other people are unpredictable, Jim feels that he must protect himself. And if he might fail, he must work extra hard to stop that from happening. Sadly, it's never enough. Nothing he does is 100%; it's just 98%!

Jim is consumed with controlling his world, and when something or someone threatens his universe, he lashes out. His controlling behaviors are serving a deeper desire for safety in a very unsafe world. His anger is what happens when he feels that his "safe" universe is being threatened.

STEP 7: MAKE THE CONNECTION

If you were a friend of Jim's then, at this point, having taken the time to get to know him, you would probably begin to show greater compassion and patience for him. God is at work in Jim's life, even though Jim may not see it. Jim needs to grasp all the truths that are his because he is united to Christ.

Over the course of our counseling, one passage that began to take root in Jim's life was 1 John 3 v 1: "See what great love the Father has lavished on us, that we should be called children of God! And that is what we are!" It addresses a core issue with Jim: Is the Father safe? Does he really care about Jim? But Jim's union with Christ has brought about his adoption by the Father.

When this verse was first read aloud to Jim, nothing really happened. But over months of rereading and meditating on it, the darkness slowly began to give way to a new light in Jim's life.

This verse became almost like a familiar friend—like a song that he would sing in his mind or under his breath. It enabled Jim to start talking to God throughout the day. He was beginning to live out his union with Christ by relating to Father, Son, and Spirit on his drive into work; as he walked from office to office at work; in his interactions with his wife and children. It also started changing the way he engaged in church life.

STEP 8: RELATE IN REAL LIFE

We often think that repentance comes before faith, but that is not necessarily the case. They play off each other like a dance. For Jim, the deep reassurance that the Father loved him engaged his heart, and he started pondering it more intently. That is faith: seeing God's love for him in Christ. This in turn enabled him to face down the things he had tended to put his trust and hope in besides Jesus. That is repentance.

This growth was further fostered in a rather unexpected place: an adult class at church where they were studying the book of Revelation. Jim had always been afraid of this book because it reminded him of God's wrath and judgment. But in the class, he started understanding that Revelation was full of encouragement! At one point he said, "My view of God is undergoing some significant shifts due to the study in Revelation. I now see that it is a letter that is written to fearful, anxious people who are facing serious persecution. The message I keep hearing is that God is in control and that he cares for his children." The picture in Revelation 19 v 6-9 of a great wedding feast, with Jesus as the bridegroom and the church as his bride, particularly stood out to him.

As these truths were becoming more real to Jim, his slavish fear of God began to dissolve, and gratitude and assurance began to grow. He was also able to begin to face his fear of others and his fear of failure. His heart was being renewed by God's greatness and compassion, and the things that he tended to trust in before began to lose their attraction. Granted, he sometimes slipped back into old ways of believing, relating to God, and behaving—but overall the change was obvious.

STEP 9: MOVE AHEAD

As Jim saw and experienced God's love and grace more and more, the persistent fear he had felt was slowly being replaced with hope that God was in control, assurance that he was loved dearly by God, gratitude for God's kindness, and finally, love for others. Here are some areas that began to slowly change.

His relationship with God was changing and so were his prayers. He really felt that he was talking to someone who was listening to him and cared for him. He wasn't alone in a vast, impersonal universe that was spinning out of control.

That changed the way he watched the news. Before, it made him terribly anxious to watch all the bad things that had happened in the world that day. It sometimes even caused a panic attack. But he became more aware of the effect that watching the news had on him, and was able to turn it off if it was working up his old fears.

Jim found that the way he drove to and from work was different. It was nothing really radical—but it was definitely different. He was still a bit nervous in big-city traffic, but his view of other drivers was changing. He was realizing their humanity. They were real people too, with lives and pressures. Jim's agitation was changing into patience. He was still vigilant behind the steering wheel, but he noticed that he was calmer. Several co-workers noticed and made a comment about how different he was in the morning when he arrived at work!

Jim's wife, who had felt as if she had to walk on eggshells around him, commented that things had improved. They still had disagreements, but Jim's fight-or-flight reactions were no longer volatile. They had marriage counseling so that they could deepen their relationship and grow in their ability to manage conflict.

Jim was more intentional about developing his relationships at church. Before, he felt that he wasn't getting anything out of the sermons, and the worship made him feel more anxious and guilty, and like a failure. Now he was seeing how he could be fed and nurtured at church and share what God was doing in his life with others.

One other significant change was seen in Jim's perfectionism. At work, he was finding it easier to let a project go, even though he knew that it was not perfect. This ability stemmed from his growing awareness that he was not a failure, and that it was therefore OK to make mistakes or not do everything perfectly. Surprisingly, Jim became more productive as he began delegating more of his work to those who reported to him.

Jim and his wife would be the first to say that this new growth was far from perfect and that it ebbed and flowed. He and his wife continued to go for marriage counseling every other week for another year until they felt that they were in a better place. Then they went every 2-3 months for a reminder and a checkup. That intentionality seemed to help them stay on course.

Today Jim's journey of change is not over. He continues to reflect on the nine steps on a regular basis. He knows he has a tendency to spiral back into old ways of thinking about God and reacting to moments of chaos in his life. He's also seeing new ways in which he wants to change and grow more like Christ.

Jim is not perfect. But with God's help, he's moving in the right direction; he's unstuck.

And with God's help, you can get unstuck too.

APPENDIX: PUT THE NINE STEPS TOGETHER

We've now covered all nine steps. But the journey isn't over: as you seek to grow in a particular area, it's helpful to regularly come back to the steps and work through them as a refresher. Use this list to easily recap on each step.

Start now by working through them with regard to the area you wrote down back on page 13. Then set a reminder in your phone or schedule to look at them again in a couple of weeks. Once you've made progress in a particular area of your life by God's grace, it might be time to focus on another one!

Get grounded: Remember who you are in Christ.

Spiritual scavenger hunt: Look for simple ways that the Spirit is already at work in your life—list ten to begin with.

Understand you: Remember how God has hard-wired you in terms of your personality and emotions. Recognize your unique strengths and vulnerabilities.

Look around: Consider your broader circumstances (body, baggage, terrain, and weather) and how they have contributed to your unique areas of vulnerability.

Gauge your reactions: Take a recent circumstance where you responded sinfully. What was going on and what did you do?

Look underneath: What did you want that you were not getting? What were you getting that you did not want?

Make the connection: Compare what you were living for in that moment with who Jesus is and the blessings that are yours right now. Is there a passage of Scripture that particularly highlights these blessings? If you can't think of one, use 1 Corinthians 1 v 30 or ask someone to help you.

Relate in real life: Based on that passage, begin to interact with God, thanking him for his love, asking him to forgive you and give you the ability to change.

Move ahead: What opportunities are there for you to love and serve others in this situation? Ask God to help you to see them.

BIBLIOGRAPHY

- Dr. Charles F. Boyd, *Different Children, Different Needs: The Art of Adjustable Parenting* (Multnomah, 1994, revised 2004)
- David Clark and Aaron T. Beck, *The Anxiety and Worry Workbook: The Cognitive Behavioral Solution* (The Guilford Press, 2012)
- Sinclair B. Ferguson, *The Christian Life: A Doctrinal Introduction* (Banner of Truth, 2013)
- Dan Goleman, *Emotional Intelligence: Why It Can Matter More Than IQ* (Bantam Books, 2005)
- William Hendriksen, *Romans* (Baker Book House, 1981)
- Timothy Keller, *Galatians For You* (The Good Book Company, 2013)
- Tim Lane, *Living Without Worry: How to Replace Anxiety with Peace* (The Good Book Company, 2015)
- C. S. Lewis, *Mere Christianity* (Macmillan, 1952)
- Gerald May, *Addiction and Grace: Love and Spirituality in the Healing of Addictions* (HarperCollins, 2009)
- John Stott, *The Message of Galatians* (IVP, 1968)

ACKNOWLEDGMENTS

This book has been brewing in my mind for over a decade. The ideas were forming as I counseled, traveled and spoke to countless churches. My primary goal was to find a way to encourage people to see that change was possible, and that what they needed was a way of connecting the lines between their daily struggles and their relationship with God. In the fall of 2016, I was invited to teach a class on worry at Carriage Lane Presbyterian Church. Near the middle of the class, as I had been mulling over *Pilgrim's Progress* by John Bunyan, it occurred to me to give the class "steps" they could take to grow in grace. Soon after that, a series of blogs began to take form that eventually shaped this book. In late 2017, the final stage came as I reconnected with The Good Book Company and pitched the idea of a book on change that was short and accessible yet nuanced enough to capture more complex struggles. They accepted my proposal and provided an excellent editor, Rachel Jones, who gave wise feedback through every iteration of each chapter.

I would like to thank each and every person who had a shaping influence on this book:

- Barbara, my wife, who is as excited as I am when I get another blog written or finish a chapter.
- My growing family: Hannah, Nate, Jesse, Tim, Kelly, Kathryn, and Ben, who regularly ask me what exactly it is that I do for a living!

- Tim Thornborough and Carl Laferton of The Good Book Company: the first ones I presented the concept to.
- Rachel Jones, for your honest, spirited and encouraging feedback. You were more than an editor; you were also a trusted friend and guide along the way.
- The marketing team at TGBC for strategizing and assisting in the graphics of the book.
- Carriage Lane Presbyterian Church of Peachtree City, Georgia, for being our home church and providing opportunities for me to serve you through opportunities to teach.
- For the many counselees who have taught me so much, and who have come to me for counsel that is grounded in the grace of the gospel and ended up teaching me as well.

My hope is that this short book would be read by individuals, couples, families, and churches. But I would also love to see it used in one-on-one discipleship relationships, and also as a foundational supplement for counselors, as you seek to help others grow in grace.

Tim Lane

ABOUT THE AUTHOR

Dr. Tim Lane is the Founder and President of the Institute for Pastoral Care, a non-profit that equips local churches to care for their people; and of Tim Lane & Associates, a counseling practice located in Peachtree City, GA. He is the author of several books on Christian living, including *How People Change*; *Relationships: A Mess Worth Making;* and *Living Without Worry: How to Replace Anxiety with Peace.* Tim is married to Barbara, and they have four grown children. Follow him on Twitter @timlane and find out more about his work or request a speaking event at www.timlane.org.

BIBLICAL | RELEVANT | ACCESSIBLE

At The Good Book Company, we are dedicated to helping Christians and local churches grow. We believe that God's growth process always starts with hearing clearly what he has said to us through his timeless word—the Bible.

Ever since we opened our doors in 1991, we have been striving to produce Bible-based resources that bring glory to God. We have grown to become an international provider of user-friendly resources to the Christian community, with believers of all backgrounds and denominations using our books, Bible studies, devotionals, evangelistic resources, and DVD-based courses.

We want to equip ordinary Christians to live for Christ day by day, and churches to grow in their knowledge of God, their love for one another, and the effectiveness of their outreach.

Call us for a discussion of your needs or visit one of our local websites for more information on the resources and services we provide.

Your friends at The Good Book Company

thegoodbook.com | thegoodbook.co.uk
thegoodbook.com.au | thegoodbook.co.nz